HAIKU

IN ENGLISH

HAIKU
IN ENGLISH
The First Hundred Years

JIM KACIAN
Editor-in-Chief

PHILIP ROWLAND AND ALLAN BURNS
Editors

With an Introduction by
BILLY COLLINS

And a Historical Overview by Jim Kacian

W. W. NORTON & COMPANY
New York | London

For information about permission to reproduce selections from this book,
write to Permissions, W. W. Norton & Company, Inc.,
500 Fifth Avenue, New York, NY 10110

For information about special discounts for bulk purchases,
please contact W. W. Norton Special Sales
at specialsales@wwnorton.com or 800-233-4830

Manufacturing by Courier Westford
Book design by Chris Welch
Production manager: Anna Oler

Library of Congress Cataloging-in-Publication Data

Haiku in English : the first hundred years / Jim Kacian, editor-in-chief ;
Philip Rowland and Allan Burns, editors ; with an introduction by Billy
Collins and a historical overview by Jim Kacian. — First edition.
        pages cm
Includes bibliographical references and index.
ISBN 978-0-393-23947-8 (hardcover)
1. Haiku. I. Kacian, Jim. II. Rowland, Philip, 1970– III. Burns, Allan
        (Allan Douglas)
        PS593.H3H35 2013
        808.81'41—dc23
                        2013014060

W. W. Norton & Company, Inc.
500 Fifth Avenue, New York, N.Y. 10110
www.wwnorton.com

W. W. Norton & Company Ltd.
Castle House, 75/76 Wells Street, London W1T 3QT

1 2 3 4 5 6 7 8 9 0

CONTENTS

ACKNOWLEDGMENTS

This project would not have been possible without the inestimable help of Charles Trumbull, whose long-term project, the Haiku Database, was the basis for much of the research we undertook, and the use of which saved us years in terms of gathering and sorting materials. We hope the database continues long into the future so later generations can benefit as well. He also provided invaluable information concerning the threads of African-American and Native American haiku that we trace in this volume.

We are grateful for the continuing support of Cor van den Heuvel, whose pioneering work in this field, though considerably different from our own, has paved the way for our contribution.

We also received significant donations of time, input, and inspiration from Richard Gilbert, who was an editor on an earlier version of this project; Alice Frampton, our chief proofreader; and Carlos Colón, with whom we consulted on "eye-ku" (visual haiku) for this volume. In addition we have benefited greatly from our collaboration with senior editor Amy Cherry, as well as with her assistant, Anna Mageras; and with Robert Weil, editor-in-chief at Liveright, who brought us together.

Billy Collins helped us reach one of our goals for the volume by providing his useful introduction. His association with this project is sure to spark much interest in haiku from the poetry mainstream, and aid in the realization of how much of a common literary heritage we share.

We would like to acknowledge the contributions our partners Maureen Gorman, Theresa Estebo, and Yuriko Rowland have made: though they have not been involved in the production of this volume, they have in a very real sense helped create the environment in which it was produced.

Finally we would like to dedicate this anthology to all the poets gathered herein who have helped to build the tradition and move the genre forward. Harold Henderson wrote that haiku will be what poets make of it: here is the fruit of that seed.

EDITORS' FOREWORD

No anthology could meet all possible criteria, and so there are several things that this volume is not. It is not a collection of all the good haiku ever written in English. Nor is it a gathering of every poet who has ever written good haiku in English. Many poets who produced creditable and even very good haiku did not get included here. It's not even an exhibit of all the best work produced by those authors who are represented. You will find poems by many of these poets that might also have been included with no loss of achievement. So what, then, is this volume, and how did we arrive at it?

Our purpose from the outset of this project has been to tell the story of English-language haiku, to identify its most singular accomplishments in its century of existence and place them, in their context, before our readers. We felt, for instance, that the order of presentation was of particular importance. You will find here the first instances we can discover of the subjects, techniques, forms, and allusions that have come to guide haiku to its present practice, and, when subsequent poems realize an even greater accomplishment, you'll find those too. You won't find, however, dozens of examples of the same sort of accomplishment, which means even some very well-known poems don't make our cut.

We also emphasized each poet's contribution to the genre, how much she or he brought to it that others could then adopt for their own work. Bashō famously wrote, "One who produces even a single good poem has not spent his life in vain." We do not take this to be hyperbole: even a single good poem is a considerable achievement, and we try to recognize it. But of course some will have done more, and we wish to recognize that as well, but all in good measure. It isn't simply that we like John Wills' or Nick Virgilio's or Raymond Roseliep's work so much more than any-one else's, it's that they broke so much new ground that proved fertile for others. We also employ a con-strained scale to regulate a poet's appearance here. Our aim was not to be exhaustive of any one poet's life's work. We know you can find completeness else-where and hope that our selections inspire you to seek out further work. Our aim was to offer what the poets themselves offered at their moments of greatest fecundity: their most original contributions, their most lasting gifts to the evolution of the genre.

At the same time, no poet produces his or her work in a vacuum. When a poet appears matters greatly to what he or she ultimately produces, and so we have chosen to order this volume not alphabetically or by date of birth of author, which are more customary, but based on the publication date of the first poem in each poet's selection—in other words, at the time he or she began making an impact on the genre. In this way the reader can come to appreciate just what a decided revolution in style John Wills' haiku were in the midst of the padded-out 5-7-5 work that was the norm at the time he began writing. Or what a breath of fresh air the humor and philosophical depth of Raymond Roseliep's work provided. Or how the formal variety of Marlene Mountain's work supplied so many new tools for poets in the genre. But such innovative success is of consequence as well: once a new means of expression has been discovered, digested, mastered, it can run its course and become stale. It has been very difficult to write a truly excellent "lily" poem after 1963, though we feel we've found a few that measure up, albeit in quite different ways. Similarly, although several good efforts at "single word in a wide white field" poems have been published since, only "tundra" is included in this volume. The challenge is not simply for other poets, either: even those who authored such innovative masterpieces are faced with the objective of surmounting themselves thereafter or merely reproducing work in modes that have already been shown to "work." For the same reason, an awareness of the interface between haiku and other short-form poetry is vital. Just as "tundra" tests a boundary between haiku and minimalist-concrete poetry, so innovative haiku have sometimes emerged from writing presented in different contexts: from the "Objectivist" (e.g., Reznikoff) to the "language-oriented" (e.g., Grenier). This haiku anthology is more inclusive than others in that respect.

2013 is a year of celebration for English-language haiku. It marks the centennial of the publication of the first fully realized haiku in English, Ezra Pound's "In a Station of the Metro," in *Poetry* magazine. Pound's poem, like no other before and few in the ensuing four decades, achieved a level of style, content, understanding, and resonance that has kept it relevant, to both modernist poetry and haiku, for a hundred years.

It also marks the golden anniversary of the founding of the first dedicated haiku journal in the English language, *American Haiku*, edited by James Bull and Don Eulert in Platteville, Wisconsin. As important as the journal was for providing a place where so many first-generation English-language haiku poets could publish, it was even more important for the model it provided to future generations. It made it seem possible that haiku could be sufficiently interesting, challenging, varied—sufficiently whole—to spawn its own poetic.

These two threads—the work of individual genius, and the building of community—supply the basic outlines for this volume. *Haiku in English* seeks to identify the achievements of the individual poet within a nurturing context unlike any other in the world of literature. The very best of these accomplishments are gathered and presented in these pages.

We arrived at our selection after a long gestation period, with the roots of this anthology going back more than a decade. We refined our concept of the book while we researched the entire oeuvres of every poet who has made a significant contribution to the development of English-language haiku. Each editor reviewed the work of assigned poets and then presented a shortlist of haiku for in-depth group discussion, which was conducted in weekly sessions via Skype while the editors sat in the comfort of their respective offices in Virginia, Colorado, and Tokyo. Only a few years earlier such a method would have been absolutely beyond a modest budget such as ours, so in a real sense the project is the product of cutting-edge technology. Yet our process remained classical: the careful consideration of words on printed pages and the give-and-take of dialectic. The research and discussions progressed chronologically, just as the book itself does, so that we could clearly gauge what achievements, departures, and continuities seemed most significant against the background of what had been accomplished each step of the way. The results reflect not the sensibility and preferences of a single editor but rather the consensus among three serious students of the genre, possessing quite distinct yet often unpredictable viewpoints. We recognize that, as with any selection, this is one of many possible takes on the subject, but it does have the special merit of years of systematic effort and investment standing behind it.

Because haiku is a living genre, its evolution will continue, and the end of this story has yet to be written. Nonetheless, we do have a clear idea of how we have arrived at this point, and it has been our goal to offer this story to you: the first hundred years.

Jim Kacian
Philip Rowland
Allan Burns

INTRODUCTION

Billy Collins

I first discovered haiku when I was in high school. The tiny genre came to me as part of my larger enchantment with Beat literature and Beat goings-on. *On the Road* was published when I was sixteen. Perfect timing. To a captive of a Catholic boys' high school in the suburbs of New York, Kerouac's novel offered a glimpse into a world of adventure involving sex, drugs, reckless driving, and bongo-playing that existed far beyond the confines of my parish. Along with Beat thinking came Zen, imported into Western culture at the time by prominent explainers such as D. T. Suzuki and Alan Watts and embraced as a daring new sensibility in Beat fiction and poetry. And along with all that came haiku. Thanks to many scholars and critics of Japanese culture, the form became widely available to English-speaking readers. One of them, Reginald Horace Blyth, who assembled a table-thumping four-volume set of traditional haiku (1949–52), thought that haiku could not be written in any language other than Japanese, but without his work as a collector and translator, haiku might not have been popularized just in time for the Beats to adopt it and give it a special American twist. Kerouac himself was a practitioner, often producing irreverent three-liners (one featuring young girls running up library steps with shorts on), though the influence of Gary Snyder brought more reflective results: Kerouac makes the memorable discovery in his medicine cabinet of a "winter fly" who has died "of old age." Kerouac also believed in "found haiku" that could be discovered embedded in other kinds of writing, claiming that there were "a million haikus in the Great Emily Dickinson." Allen Ginsberg considered Kerouac's *The Dharma Bums* a novel "of a thousand haiku." One contemporary blogger has even tried to locate and catalogue all of that book's hidden "haikus." It seems that unintentional haiku can be found anywhere if you bother to look and listen. I myself have overheard accidental haiku in such unlikely places as a school hallway and a supermarket aisle.

Fascinated by the Beats and full of what little I understood of Buddhism, I began to commit my own acts of haiku, managing to contribute some unwitting travesties to the ancient and honorable tradition.

Of course, at the time I was too taken with the notion that my three-liners gave me something in common with the Village hipsters and the enlightened monks in the temples of Japan to recognize my poems were failures. I had not yet heard that even some Zen masters consider one bull's-eye out of thirty haiku attempts a decent average. It might well have been such a comment that brought my haiku-writing to a halt. But decades later, I took it up again in earnest shortly after I decided to get another dog.

The dog was a mixed-breed female I found at an animal rescue center. Her lineage—if that's not too elevated a word—was anyone's guess, but she looked a lot like an Australian shepherd, and sometimes she would try to herd me around the house by the ankles. I named her Jeannine after a jazz-played tune by Cannonball Adderley. She was such a pretty dog.

Soon after she was trained to be off-leash, I got in the habit of walking with her every morning along the shore of a nearby reservoir, and almost every morning I would try to compose a haiku before we got back home, the "season word" changing with the seasons. Humans might value a walk as exercise, but for dogs a walk is an opportunity to gather information. While the dog sniffed the ground, I counted syllables on my fingers. While she read the recent canine news, I tried to fit some little insight into a seventeen-syllable box. Somewhat like the anonymous Irish monk who wrote a poem about his cat Pangur Ban and their mutually diligent pursuits—the monk pursuing learning, the cat pursuing mice—I was looking for one thing on our walk and the dog for another. I once tried to shuffle together our parallel enterprises:

> The dog stops to sniff
> the poems of others
> before she recites her own.

Along with the outbreak of haiku in America in the 1950s came the Great Seventeen-Syllable Debate, which continues to simmer in the haiku community to this day. Many poets, myself included, stick to the basic form of seventeen syllables, typically arranged in three lines in a 5-7-5 order. This light harness is put on like any formal constraint in poetry so the poet can feel the comfort of its embrace while being pushed by those same limits into unexpected discoveries. Asked where he got his inspiration, Yeats answered, "in looking for the next rhyme word." To follow such rules, whether received as is the case with the sonnet or concocted on the spot, is to feel the form pushing back against one's self-expressive impulses. For the poet, this palpable resistance can be a vital part of the compositional experience. I count syllables not out of any allegiance to tradition but because I want the indifference and inflexibility of a seventeen-syllable limit to balance my self-expressive yearnings. With the form in place, the act of composition becomes a negotiation between one's subjective urges and the rules of order, which in this case could not be simpler or firmer. My hope is that such fixity will keep the pulsations of the ego in check by encouraging a degree of humility in the face of the form.

These days, many haiku poets—in fact, the large majority—ignore the syllable count. They stand by the linguistic fact that a "syllable" does not have the same meaning or weight in Japanese as it does in English. Writing in the early days of the American Haiku, Kerouac pointed out this difference: "The American Haiku is not exactly the Japanese Haiku. The Japanese Haiku is strictly disciplined to seventeen syllables but since the language structure is different I don't think American Haikus (short three-line poems intended to be completely packed with Void of Whole) should worry about syllables because American speech is something again . . . bursting to pop. Above all, a haiku must be very simple and free of poetic trickery and make a little picture and yet be as airy and graceful as a Vivaldi Pastorella." Whether they are the counting or the non-counting type, poets are likely to agree that at the heart of the haiku lies something beyond counting, that is, its revelatory effect on the reader, that eye-opening moment of insight that occurs whenever a haiku succeeds in drawing us through the keyhole of its details into the infinite, or to put it more ineffably, into the "Void of the Whole." No one would argue that any tercet that mentions a cloud or a frog qualifies as a real haiku; it would be like calling an eleven-line poem about courtly love a sonnet. A true haiku contains a special uncountable feature, and every serious devotee of the form aims to achieve that with every attempt.

As we now turn to the collection in hand, *Haiku in English: The First Hundred Years*, I'd like to stress this "pop" quality of haiku, that epiphanic jolt, the "Aha!" moment.

Haiku is both easy and impossible to define. One can merely use dictionary language to say that a haiku is a short poem, usually in three lines that uses natural imagery to evoke a feeling or mood. But such flat definitions fall well short of accounting for haiku's mysterious power to cause in the reader's consciousness a sudden shift, literally a new way of seeing. Part of this ability lies in the form's brevity, which leaves no time to explain an experience; instead, the haiku conveys an experience directly without commentary and with an immediacy not possible in longer poems. Wordworth's famous daffodil poem for all its charm is a good example of a non-haiku. True, the speaker enjoys an elevated experience in nature, which he conveys with excitement ("A host of golden daffodils . . ."), but in the end he looks back on the experience and tells us what it meant, how it moved him from loneliness to "the bliss of solitude." Central to the poem is a moment of haiku-like attention ("I gazed—and gazed—but little thought . . ."), a gazing that is perception raised to the second power; but the length of the daffodil poem, its use of simile (comparing the flowers to the stars in the "milky way"), and its meditative conclusion are in stark contrast to the bare, stripped-down simplicity of haiku.

Like the practitioners of any verse form, haiku poets have a number of techniques at their disposal. One way single moments are endowed with surprising significance is through juxtaposition. While traditional Western poetry uses simile and metaphor to make comparisons, haiku wants to present the world just as it is. When we compare things, we are saying that this is like that, but in haiku, nothing is like anything else. Things are simply what they are; the blossom, the river, the cup are simply themselves—self-sufficient, unadorned, free of literary embellishment. The moon is not like a wafer; the moon is the moon. To say it's a wafer is to distract from the "moonness" of the moon. Instead of using comparisons, the haiku simply positions things next to each other. The startling effects that can result are based not on analogies but on immediate connections. "A page of Shelley / brightens and dims / with passing clouds"), "jackknifed rig / a trooper waves us / into wildflowers." The contrast is often between the natural and the man-made, for example "in the stream / a shopping cart / fills with leaves." The natural world sometimes lies next to the world of human activities as in "I lay down / all the heavy packages— / autumn moon." That same "looking up" can create a shift so abrupt as to suggest a printer's error: "looking up / rules of punctuation— / green hills." Whether you call this maneuver a "cut" (*kire*), a pivot (*kake kotoba*), or an imaginative leap, the effect is surprise followed by eye-widening awareness: "after the garden party / the garden."

In some juxtapositions the small is set beside the large, the lowly next to the grand: "Moonlit sleet / In the holes of my / Harmonica," "Through the slats / of the outhouse door / Everest!" "The morning paper— / I set down my coffee cup / in Buenos Aires." The effect is a kind of Alice-in-Wonderland dislocation of our size-logic that causes the relative meanings of Big and Tiny to fall away. The sun touches your refrigerator; midwinter visits a dollhouse; stars reach from your house to your barn. Each connection implies that the micro and the macro are both part of the great sensorium, the world of sense impressions that envelops our every waking hour.

A haiku moment may result from a misperception, a wrong-seeing. What seems to be a fallen leaf returning miraculously to a branch turns out to be a rising butterfly. Clever optical illusions may occur: "The fleeing sandpipers / turn about suddenly / and chase back the sea!" As well as visual surprises: "passport check / my shadow waits / across the border." And strange animations: "Winter burial: / a stone angel points his hand / at the empty sky" and "wood pile / on the sagging porch / unstacking itself."

A haiku feeling may arise from emptiness, absence, and silence. Just as the spaces in music are as important as the notes, so what is not there is as potent as what is: "an empty elevator / opens / closes," "before we enter / after we leave / the meditation room."

What is missing can even be palpable: "all day long / I feel its weight / the unworn necklace." A surfboard in the waves without a rider, an empty swing still moving in a playground—these empty spaces suggest our own possible absence; being alone (*sabi*) can make us wonder where everyone went. The haiku can take us from lightness into nothingness and make us aware of the little voids around us and the great voids that precede and follow time itself.

As Shakespeare broke the hold that courtly love had on the sonnet by introducing new subject matter, many haiku poets today are testing the elasticity of the form by using non-traditional subjects having nothing to do with the natural world: "bearing down / on a borrowed pen / do not resuscitate." The form also seems to welcome parody and ironic deflation. Well-known is Richard Brautigan's "Haiku Ambulance": in which a piece of green pepper falls out of a salad bowl. The poet's reaction is "So what?" More subtle is "out of the haze / the dog brings back / the wrong stick." Here's my own contribution: "Flying with a twig / a bird disappears into / the town's noon siren." And here's a seventeen-syllable gem by Paul Violi that you should not share with your bank teller: "Don't look at my face. / No change, just large bills. / One wrong move will be your last."

Many people don't get haiku. They typically ask what the big deal is about a frog leaping into a pond or a piece of green pepper falling off a salad bowl. So what indeed? Maybe the best answer is a slap on the face, a common "answer" to a baffling koan. But a more reasonable explanation of the "big deal" is the irreducible fact that the poet was there to witness the event. A cherry tree in blossom and a dog barking in the distance may not seem to add up to much, but what such a haiku declares is that someone was present—actually there, living and breathing—at that particular intersection of sight and sound. In that sense, haiku not only convey the beauty of individually experienced moments, they are also powerful little assertions of the poet's very existence. Not to be present to witness the cherry tree and the barking dog means being absent, perhaps non-existent. Every haiku makes a common claim: I was there! Like Kilroy with his nose over the fence.

The best haiku contain a moment in time caught in the amber of the poet's attention and the poem's words. It is the only genre fully devoted to setting down a simple observation in the here-and-now so as to produce in the reader a little gasp. In honoring small events by italicizing moments in time, haiku should remind us of the multitude of forgotten moments, past and present, that surround each perfectly arrested one. The stop-time instant at the heart of haiku might be said to offer resistance to the remorseless powers of forgetfulness.

It may not be very "haiku" of me to compare haiku to anything else, but I want to end by stretching an analogy between haiku and physics. Just as matter is composed of atoms, which give off a great energy when accelerated to the point of collision, so time is made up of moments; and when a single moment is perfectly isolated, another kind of cosmic energy is released. I like to think of the haiku as a moment-smashing device out of which arise powerful moments of dazzling awareness. But I also like to think of it as a something to do while walking the dog.

HAIKU
IN ENGLISH

EZRA POUND

IN A STATION OF THE METRO

The apparition of these faces in the crowd;
Petals on a wet, black bough.

TS'AI CHI'H

The petals fall in the fountain,
        the orange-coloured rose-leaves,
Their ochre clings to the stone.

FAN-PIECE, FOR HER IMPERIAL LORD

O Fan of white silk,
        clear as frost on the grass-blade,
You also are laid aside.

WALLACE STEVENS

(from "Thirteen Ways of Looking at a Blackbird")

I

Among twenty snowy mountains,
The only moving thing
Was the eye of the blackbird.

IX

When the blackbird flew out of sight,
It marked the edge
Of one of many circles.

Mid-Summer Dusk

Swallows twittering at twilight:
Waves of heat
Churned to flames by the sun.

AMY LOWELL

Last night it rained.
Now, in the desolate dawn,
Crying of blue jays.

Nuance

Even the iris bends
When a butterfly lights upon it.

CHARLES REZNIKOFF

About an excavation
a flock of bright red lanterns
has settled.

Aphrodite Urania

the ceaseless weaving of the uneven water

YVOR WINTERS

WINTER ECHO

Thin air! My mind is gone.

Suicide's Note

The calm,
Cool face of the river
Asked me for a kiss.

Snow man
snow woman
melting away in the sun.

walking through the forest
I rearrange
the trees

cobwebs
hesitating
us

E. E. CUMMINGS

l(a

le

af

fa

ll

s)

one

li

ness

ALLEN GINSBERG

Mayan head in a
Pacific driftwood bole
—Someday I'll live in N.Y.

The madman
emerges from the movies:
the street at lunchtime.

Moonless thunder—yellow dandelions flash in fields
of rainy grass.

GARY SNYDER

This morning:
                   floating face down in the water bucket
     a drowned mouse

         the boulder in the creek never moves
         the water is always falling
         together!

JACK KEROUAC

Missing a kick
at the icebox door
It closed anyway

Empty baseball field
—A robin,
Hops along the bench

Straining at the padlock,
the garage doors
At noon

Evening coming—
the office girl
unloosing her scarf

The bottoms of my shoes
  are clean
From walking in the rain

In my medicine cabinet
the winter fly
Has died of old age

Useless! Useless!
—heavy rain driving
into the sea

Thunder in the mountains—
the iron
of my mother's love

RICHARD WRIGHT

The sudden thunder
Startles the magnolias
To a deeper white.

In the falling snow
A laughing boy holds out his palms
Until they are white.

The indentation
Made by her head on the pillow:
A heavy snowfall.

Coming from the woods,
A bull has a lilac sprig
    Dangling from a horn.

Just enough of rain
To bring the smell of silk
    From umbrellas.

One autumn evening
A stranger enters a village
    And passes on through.

COR VAN DEN HEUVEL

snow
on the saddle-bags
sun in skull

the shadow in the folded napkin

hot day
the mime leans into a wind
that isn't there

an empty wheelchair
rolls
in from the waves

the windy stars—
the distant gas station lights
go out

city street
the darkness inside
the snow-covered cars

tundra

lingering snow
the game of catch continues
into evening

changing pitchers
the runner on first looks up
at a passing cloud

end of the line
the conductor starts turning
the seats around

Searching on the wind,
the hawk's cry . . .
is the shape of its beak

Bitter morning:
sparrows sitting
without necks.

Deep within the stream
the huge fish lie motionless,
facing the current.

Half of the minnows
   within this sunlit shallow
     are not really there.

The fleeing sandpipers
   turn about suddenly
     and chase back the sea!

Tightening the sky
   already taut with gray:
     a slow-wheeling hawk

O MABSON SOUTHARD

The old rooster crows . . .
   Out of the mist come the rocks
   and the twisted pine

One breaker crashes . . .
   As the next draws up, a lull—
   and sandpiper cries

Down to dark leaf-mold
   the falling dogwood petal
   carries its moonlight

CLEMENT HOYT

Leaves moil in the yard,
   reveal an eyeless doll's head . . .
    slowly conceal it.

A Hallowe'en mask,
   floating face up in the ditch,
    slowly shakes its head.

NICK VIRGILIO

lily:
out of the water . . .
out of itself

bass
picking bugs
off the moon

over spatterdocks,
turning at corners of air:
dragonfly

fossilence

flag-covered coffin:
the shadow of the bugler
slips into the grave

removing
   the bulletproof vest:
      the heat

autumn twilight:
   the wreath on the door
      lifts in the wind

my dead brother . . .
hearing his laugh
in my laughter

Easter morning . . .
the sermon is taking the shape
of her neighbor's hat

the sack of kittens
sinking in the icy creek
increases the cold

spentagon
pentagony
repentagon

town barberpole
stops turning:
autumn nightfall

barking its breath
into the rat-hole:
bitter cold

after the bell,
within the silence:
within myself

DAG HAMMARSKJÖLD

In the castle's shadow
the flowers closed
long before evening.

GERALD ROBERT VIZENOR

After the heavy rains
So many skies tonight
Reflecting the moon.

cedar cones
tumble in a mountain stream
letters from home

JOHN TAGLIABUE

A child looking at
    ants; an elephant looking
    at universes.

CID CORMAN

On the brim of a
brimming stone bowl a
stone.

Dark morning.
Snow?

Yes
after no.

Of one stone: chariot charioteer
horses harness reins and the Victory.

Small Song

The reeds give
way to the

wind and give
the wind away

JULIUS LESTER

As we got
Closer, the
Rainbow disappeared.

BERNARD LIONEL EINBOND

the white of her neck
as she lifts her hair for me
to undo her dress

TOM RAWORTH

now the melody
in the pattern of shadows
one shadow behind

ROBERT SPIESS

A fine sleet at dusk;
    mallards in the marshy cove
      float beneath their wings

Blue jays in the pines;
    the northern river's ledges
      cased with melting ice

Dry, summer day;
    chalk-white plover mute
      on a mid-stream rock

a round melon
    in a field of round melons
      —resting dragonfly

No wind
　　the chrysalis
　　　trembles

Lean-to of tin;
　　a pintail on the river
　　　in the pelting rain

Skull of a horse—
　　the painter's brush returning it
　　　to the desert sand

Muttering thunder . . .
　　the bottom of the river
　　　scattered with clams

Becoming dusk,—
   the catfish on the stringer
   swims up and down

the field's evening fog—
   quietly the hound comes
   to fetch me home

JACK CAIN

an empty elevator
opens
closes

GARY HOTHAM

fog.
sitting here
without the mountains

distant thunder
the dog's toenails click
against the linoleum

deserted tennis court
  wind through the net

waiting room quiet
an apple core
in the ashtray

clouds move in
under the clouds
moving out

yesterday's paper
in the next seat—
the train picks up speed

coffee
in a paper cup—
a long way from home

she comes back—
the ocean drips off
every part of her

evening loon call—
nothing makes it
call again

letting
the dog out—
the stars out

WILLIAM J. HIGGINSON

Holding the water
held by it—
the dark mud.

I look up
from writing
to daylight.

JOHN WILLS

dusk   from rock to rock a waterthrush

    mule
    dragging dawn
    across the ridge

the sun lights up a distant ridge   another

    the hills
    release the summer clouds
    one   by one   by one

den of the bear
beyond the great rocks
storm clouds

keep out sign
but the violets keep on
going

the moon at dawn
lily pads blow white
in a sudden breeze

rain in gusts
below the deadhead
troutswirl

this rock
in moonlight   warmer
than the others

a snowy owl
swoops in and turns
the snow gray

a box of nails
on the shelf in the shed
the cold

boulders
just beneath the boat
it's dawn

going
where the river goes
first day of spring

wildflowers:
letting the years
slip away

ROD WILLMOT

Listening . . .
After a while,
    I take up my axe again

the water stills:
a crayfish enters
        the hollows of my face

A page of Shelley
brightens and dims
            with passing clouds

the mirror fogs,
a name written long ago
faintly reappears

VIRGINIA BRADY YOUNG

On the first day of spring
snow falling
from one bough to another.

Vaster
than the prairie—
this wind.

at twilight
hippo
      shedding
      the river

white lilacs
before sunrise
their own light

MICHAEL MCCLINTOCK

the dead
come apart:
downpour
   (from "Vietnam: Poems")

pushing
      inside . . . until
            her teeth shine

while we wait
to do it again,
the rains of spring

where three drowned
the lake water
sparkles in the morning

moonrise . . .
eyes of rock mice
rim the dry gully

60 stories
of glass:
the summer moon

dead cat . . .
open-mouthed
to the pouring rain

Somewhere behind me,
seeming in dark-silence
to feel a slow coiling.

MICHAEL SEGERS

in the eggshell after the chick has hatched

passing whale's eye . . .
the islands on the horizon
sink and rise again

GGGGGGGGGGGGGGGGGGGGGGG
RRRRRRESRRRRRRRRRRRRRR
AAAAAKSNAAAAAAAASNAAAA
SSNKESSKESSSSSSSNAKESS
SSAKESSSESNSSSSSAKESSS
GGGGGGGGGNAKGGGAKEGGGG
RRRRRRRRRRKESRAKERRRRR
AAAAAAAAAAASNAKEAAAAAA
SSSSSSSSSSSSAKESSSSSSS
SSSSSSSSSSSSSSSSSSSSSS

sound of honking geese
deep in the mirror
a very small door

GERALDINE CLINTON LITTLE

Fallen horse—
flies hovering
in the vulture's shadow

the daisies
you paint full
of philosophy

LARRY WIGGIN

cleaning whelks
the sound
of the knife

crickets . . .
then
thunder

DAVID LLOYD

Moonlit sleet
In the holes of my
Harmonica

L. A. DAVIDSON

what to say?
  forced forsythia
  on a winter day

the surfboard riding a wave in by itself

beyond
stars beyond
  star

LORRAINE ELLIS HARR

A hot summer wind—
   shadows of the windmill blades
      flow over the grass.

an owl hoots darkness down from the hollow oak

Midwinter gloom—
she turns on the lights
in her doll's house

Moving
　　through the criteria—
　　　　　a breeze.

moths have come
around the one light left
forgotten, on

they wade in, and
　　suddenly the moon's out
　　　with their arms

moving out tomorrow
their
sounds now

the long night
of the mannequins—
snow falling

bolted   space

the lights on the corners
click and change

when the suicide
        cut out
    that sky

terminal.
one far off
and perfect moon

JANICE BOSTOK

stationary bus—
talking we visit places
within each other

a fox in daylight chasing and being chased by crows

pregnant again . . .
the fluttering of moths
against the window

foetus kicks
the sky to the east
brilliant

tiny coffin
the long winter
's passing

ALAN PIZZARELLI

meteor

the cloud fades back
into blackness

snow piles up
the barber shop pole
spins into itself

driving
out of the car wash

clouds move
across the hood

in the stream
   a shopping cart
      fills with leaves

twilight
staples rust
in the telephone pole

a spark
falls to the ground
      darkens

that's it

ELIZABETH SEARLE LAMB

pausing
halfway up the stair—
white chrysanthemums

in the hot sun
still   swinging
  this empty swing

a lizard inching
with the shadow of the stone
nearer the cave's mouth

cry of the peacock   the crack in the adobe wall

                    the emptiness
            where the eyes were in the shed
                                    snakeskin

            glissandos
            rippling from the strings
            wind from the sea

            dust from the ore tailings
            a flash of tanager wings
            in the hot sun

            the sound
            of rain on the sound
            of waves

MARLENE MOUNTAIN

pig and i spring rain

on this cold
      spring   1
    2 night 3 4
      kittens
       wet
        5

wood pile
on the sagging porch
unstacking itself

thrush song a few days before the thrush

he leans on the gate going staying

one fly everywhere the heat

above the mountain mountains of the moon

a butterfly december rises to meet it

spin on dead and wounded any scratch of pines

less and less nature is nature

old pond a frog rises belly up

RICHARD WILBUR

Sleepless at Crown Point

All night, this headland
Lunges into the rumpling
Capework of the wind.

RAYMOND ROSELIEP

birthcry!
    the stars
    are all in place

after childbirth
she wants to see
the withered moor

her hourglass figure
in
my father's watch

the wren
moves apart
from its song

flea . . .
that you,
Issa?

he removes his glove
        to point out
                Orion

after Beethoven
he gets the furnace
roaring

the space
between the deer
and the shot

i.v. dripping;
the chipping sparrow's
one pitch

with his going
the birds go
nameless

downpour:
my "I-Thou"
T-shirt

ordering my tombstone:
the cutter has me feel
his Gothic "R"

snow
all's
new

GEORGE SWEDE

at the edge of the precipice   I grow logical

dawn
remembering her
bad grammar

passport check
my shadow waits
across the border

the son who
argues everything
I study his face
in a puddle

   wildflowers
I cannot name
  most of me

at the height
of the argument   the old couple
pour each other tea

Turning everything
into itself
the wind

one by one to the floor all of her shadows

alone at last
i wonder where
everyone is

JEFFREY WINKE

blue dusk
  turning sand dunes
  into snow

MATSUO ALLARD

alone at 3:00 a.m.—the door knob turning slowly

an icicle the moon drifting through it

deep in my notebook a lily pad floats away

higher this time the last salmon

BETTY DREVNIOK

Morning coolness:
even the river's sounds
are fog . . .

RUTH YARROW

after the garden party   the garden

flash on the rim—
side canyon prolonging
thunder

my thumbprint
on this thousand-year-old pot
fits hers

a marmot's whistle
pierces the mountain
first star

the baby's pee
pulls roadside dust
into rolling beads

warm rain before dawn:
my milk flows into her
unseen

new leaf—
a tiny beetle chews a hole
to the sky

ROBERT GRENIER

except the swing bumped by the dog in passing

GÜNTHER KLINGE

Indian summer.
Even a small affection
has its urgency.

ROBERT BOLDMAN

walking with the river
     the water does my thinking

lark song
down to
its bones

in the pines
my spine
straightens

visible lilacs
shaped by
invisible lilacs

leaves blowing into a sentence

Death camp in the photograph
the little girl's hair will always be blowing

in the doll's
head
news clippings

face wrapping a champagne glass

the priest
          his shadow caught
     on a nail .

PEGGY WILLIS LYLES

before we knew its name the indigo bunting

I brush
my mother's hair
the sparks

thunderheads offshore
the osprey coming early
to its nest

darker
than the mind's eye
crows in summer grass

dragonfly . . .
the tai chi master
shifts his stance

Indian summer
a turtle on a turtle
on a rock

reaching for green pears—
the pull
of an old scar

equinox
a new teacher
adjusts the globe

summer night:
we turn out all the lights
to hear the rain

JOHN ASHBERY

A blue anchor grains of grit in a tall sky sewing

I inch and only sometimes as far as the twisted pole
    gone in spare colors

Too late the last express passes through the dust of
    gardens

cloudberries:
tasting
the word

lunar eclipse
your body
in the sea's motion

body bag
not asking
not telling

between fugues
the sound of rain
on stained-glass

from winter storage
   the prow of the canoe
      entering sunlight

ALEXIS ROTELLA

Late August—
I bring him the garden
in my skirt.

At the top
of the ferris wheel,
lilac scent.

across the paper they follow my brush geese

Undressed—
today's role dangles
from a metal hanger.

Trying to forget him—
stabbing
the potatoes.

PAUL O. WILLIAMS

a cat watches me
across the still pond,
across our difference

from mud
    to sky
        the heron's feet

after the zinnias
the gardener, too,
drinks from the hose

tree
by tree
the summer fog

gone from the woods
the bird I knew
by song alone
(for Nick Virgilio)

spring the one dead tree

JAMES KIRKUP

walking in dead leaves—
sending the sparrows flying
further down the path

the blood of my shadow poured up the steps

In atomic rain
Buddha goes on smiling at
the last butterfly

After the drama
　Of delicate stored secretions,
　　Soothing flatness.

CHUCK BRICKLEY

manhole steam
two men with briefcases
from the other world

on his youth in Japan
my neighbor falls silent . . .
the clear summer sky

the last rays
a man hurls a starfish
back into the sea

KENNETH REXROTH

As the full moon rises
The swan sings
In sleep
On the lake of the mind.

SCOTT MONTGOMERY

her silence at dinner
sediment
        hanging in the wine

NICK AVIS

the telephone
rings only once
       autumn rain

she raises the hem
of her new dress
the day now longer

northern lights shimmer
       a saw-whet piping
       on the distant shore

deep inside the faded wood a scarlet maple

freshly fallen snow
                    opening a new package
            of typing paper

PENNY HARTER

evening rain—
I braid my hair
into the dark

broken bowl
the pieces
still rocking

the war memorial—
migrating butterflies
cover the names

RUBY SPRIGGS

moment of birth new shadow

inukshuk
   sunshadow
      moonshadow

my head in the clouds in the lake

LARRY EIGNER

one of two nickels

a fly walking the rim
    makes it flicker, shine

glad to have
these copies of things
after a while

politics

        suspended in snow

MATTHEW LOUVIÈRE

Through the weave
in the gunny sack
—crabs spittling stars

saying too much
the deaf girl
hides her hands

WALLY SWIST

dewy morning:
the logging truck's load
sweating sap

walking farther into it
the farther it moves away
spring mist

mourning dove
answers mourning dove—
coolness after the rain

heat lightning
the screams
of mating raccoons

deep bend of the brook
    the kingfisher's chatter
after its dive

shadow after shadow
the flock of migrating geese
passing through us

MARGARET CHULA

Hiroshima heat
mother and daughter
fold a thousand cranes

night of the new moon
I crave nothing, no one
frogs croaking, croaking

Through the slats
of the outhouse door
Everest!

WINONA BAKER

moss-hung trees
a deer moves into
the hunter's silence

Dangerous pavements . . .
But this year I face the ice
with my father's stick

CHARLES B. DICKSON

rain-swept parking lot
headlights of a locked car
grow dim

November field
a birddog sculptured
by the scent of quail

shrill midnight cries
of low-flying snow geese
a meteor flares

dense fog
a mockingbird
fills it

the narcissus opens:
nothing to believe,
     nothing to doubt

H. F. "TOM" NOYES

Monday morning—
a flaw in the shadow
of the sugar bowl

Religion aside
there are plum blossoms
and pussy willows

arguing a point—
the tug with its haul of logs
gone out of sight

ANNE MCKAY

a flame set to fit the need between yes and no . . .

a rook in a nave of light
the weave
         of a night river

my words
  yellow
  ochre
  umber
        in lieu of jonquils

deep into the rainy valley
the ghostcamp
        home again of marten and raven

PATRICIA DONEGAN

I lay down
all the heavy packages—
autumn moon.

last night lightning
this morning
the white iris

spring wind—
I too
am dust

An empty plate
Smashing it

Autumn clearer

ANN ATWOOD

dead center
in the center of her flowers
Georgia O'Keeffe

DEE EVETTS

thunder
my woodshavings roll
along the veranda

after Christmas
a flock of sparrows
in the unsold trees

custody battle
a bodyguard lifts the child
to see the snow

his fury
pulled up short
by the payphone cord

damp morning
cash for a journey
warm from the machine

deep in the mountains
the shaving mirror
shows me the mountains

the river
            going over
the afternoon
going on

GARRY GAY

Hunter's moon:
the raccoon washing something
in the river

Bird song:
the color
of dawn

Along the way
an old oak branch
becomes a walking stick

Skunk skull
the smell
of a summer shower

The shape of clay
   before
      she makes it something

Navajo moon
the coyote call
not a coyote

In the back alley,
one light . . .
the old snow

HAL ROTH

dove song shortens the lane to where she waits

LEE GURGA

fresh scent—
    the labrador's muzzle
      deeper into snow

spot of sunlight—
on a blade of grass the dragonfly
changes its grip

rows of corn
stretch to the horizon—
sun on the thunderhead

from house
to barn:
the milky way

not
the
whole
story
but probably enough
fresh
snow

an unspoken assumption tracks through the petals

FRANK K. ROBINSON

anzio beach . . .
another wave gathers
and breaks

MICHAEL FESSLER

reaching the top
of the mountain
losing the mountain

rain hits a clear
plastic umbrella
fear of documents

MICHAEL DYLAN WELCH

after the quake
    the weathervane
        pointing to earth

morning chill . . .
the bag of marbles
shifts on the shelf

paper route
    knocking a row of icicles
    from the eave

pulsing
in the wiper's blade
the bee's abdomen

crackling beach fire—
we hum in place of words
we can't recall

meteor shower . . .
a gentle wave
wets our sandals

VINCENT TRIPI

Her only nipple
begins to harden
a new year

Changing the swallowtail
    changed by it
        the spring wind

Sun
    in the bee's compound eye
        on the sunflower

Not falling
       caterpillar
           on the falling leaf

Ah water-strider never to have left a track!

Colouring itself across the pond the autumn wind . . .

Deathbed . . .
       my old friend's imitation
           of a firefly

The shell I take,
the shell it takes
—ebb tide

In
    his silence too
      jazz

(for Jeremy Starpoli)

BILL PAULY

snowmelt . . .
she enters
the earth on her knees

back from the war
all his doors
swollen shut

DAVID COBB

filling the grave
more earth
than will go back in

spring sunshine
my dead wife's handprints
on the window pane

sciatica—
I listen to the lark
flat out

the old spin bowler
fingers busy
with a bowl of sloes

a moment between
lighthouse flashes
cold smell of fish

a bust of wet clay—
feeling one's own face
from the inside

daffodil morning—
looking for something
very blue to wear

JERRY BALL

spring breeze
archers at their targets
collecting arrows

autumn evening . . .
as we stare at the planets
a stranger joins us

JOHN BRANDI

fallen leaves
the abbot sweeps
around them

a party
where everyone says goodbye
then stays

DAVID ELLIOTT

among leafless trees
    too many thoughts
    in my head

LEROY GORMAN

between
Goethe & Graves
summer
shelfdust

in the silent movie
a bird I think extinct
is singing

quiet graveyard
warm breeze and an end
to alphabetic order

PETER YOVU

the mountain path
winding up
at a snail

an unseen bird sings
     the dew is red is green is
       blue

she slips into
the ocean the ocean
slips into

October
the red shift
you were buried in

a falcon dives
how completely
I surround my bones

at the brink
wind that brought me here
      goes on

CHRISTOPHER HEROLD

foghorns . . .
we lower a kayak
into the sound

fields flooded—
beneath the surface, somewhere,
the river bends

chimney smoke
moonlight changing direction
with the wind

shooting star—
abruptly the campfire
rekindles itself

Sierra sunrise . . .
pine needles sink deeper
in a patch of snow

bird shadow
    from tree shadow
        to fence shadow

elevator silence—
our eyes escape
into numbers

    before we enter
    after we leave
the meditation room

JANE REICHHOLD

autumn
taking a dirt road
to the end

mountain echo
I'm older
when I hear it

a piece of night
breaks off to strike
a scorpion

STEVE SANFIELD

The earth shakes
just enough
to remind us.

MARIAN OLSON

stars
        before letting go
letting go

who was here first
        the crack deepens
in the adobe wall

scattering seed the cock all claws

river's song
a wounded turtle
slips into it

god or no god
does it matter
wild blue flax

whole as the snakeskin surrender

winter sun
you choose to die
with a shrug

JIM KACIAN

the river
the river makes
of the moon

clouds seen
through clouds
seen through

walking in
the orchard suddenly
its   plan

camping alone one star then many

i hope i'm right where the river ice ends

gunshot the length of the lake

long view to Sirius even the past isn't past

pain fading the days back to wilderness

swallowflight . . .
looking out the window
long after

my fingerprints
on the dragonfly
in amber

whittling
till there's nothing left
of the light

EBBA STORY

edge of the marsh—
the wind from rising geese
in our hair

through thinning mist
distant sunlit breakers:
the nurse calls my name

closing
the hinge of space between us
      the kinglet's eye

BRUCE ROSS

sunny afternoon
all the fire engines gone from
the open bays

coming to rest
the tossed pebble
takes a shadow

Thoreau's gravesite:
the smell of woodsmoke
on the cold spring air

ARIZONA ZIPPER

a shallow grave
in the ferns, gnats rise and fall
on a spoke of sun

CHERIE HUNTER DAY

salt wind ripples on an inner lake

palominos—
curve of the winter hills
in moonlight

a skull no bigger
than my thumbnail
jasmine in bloom

talk of the war
a spider shedding
its pale replica

looking up
rules of punctuation—
the green hills

winding road
for the next eight miles
Coltrane

termites
with temporary wings
the debt ceiling

MIKE DILLON

accidental orchard: I am found

the beautiful nun
doesn't see me:
summer noon

The last kid picked
running his fastest
to right field

it doesn't matter
what I think:
Milky Way

CARLOS COLÓN

pointing
my way home
the starfish

overtaken
by weeds
the road not taken

closing arguments
the length of the lawyer's
skirt

CAROLINE GOURLAY

fog-bound road—
walking on the inside of
the inside world

again no word . . .
on the map only inches
to your island shore

daylight fading—
a curlew's cry
lengthens the hill

unopened letter—
a kestrel hovers
in the distance

without a full stop
you run—childhood, a country
with no paragraphs

WILLIAM M. RAMSEY

fate: a leaf falls   but with improvisation

slave cemetery
i scrape the moss to find
no name

what sadness—
the rose bloom is perfect
   just now

   curtains rippling
her pillow
   wild with hair

   confronting the dark
a firefly
   illumines its guts

JOHN STEVENSON

a deep gorge . . .
some of the silence
is me

one last look
through the old apartment
a dry sponge

jampackedelevatoreverybuttonpushed

cold moon—
a moment of hesitation
years ago

last piece
of a jigsaw puzzle . . .
filling in the sky

the spell check questions them:
Majdanek, Sobibor,
Belzec . . .

snowy night
sometimes you can't be
quiet enough

nothing matters how green it gets

curling tighter
a leaf
catches fire

ROBERT MAINONE

Firefly garden . . .
rising up
to fill the sky

my haplogroup
shows the sponge gene—
distant lightning

MARTIN LUCAS

somewhere
between
Giggleswick and Wigglesworth
I am uninspired

the thyme-scented morning lizard's tongue flicking out

facing fine rain
on the upturned boat
a heron, hunched

greener than autumn light
   on wind-bent reeds
      the teal's wing

long shadows
through the quiet schoolyard
the killdeer's cry

CHRIS GORDON

a love letter to
the butterfly gods with
strategic misspellings

I meet the twin she
never mentioned the mist
lit briefly by the sun

the nickels from
your pocket are cold
a few small wars

a purple evening in the window she folds her
   underwear

the hand that always aches talking to a girl about
   long division

where the lines end and the absence begins an
   architecture or so

PATRICIA NEUBAUER

New Year's parade—
beneath the dancing dragon
the feet of men

ROBERT GILLILAND

autumn wind—
a brown bag still holding
the bottle's shape

jackknifed rig
a trooper waves us
into wildflowers

morning bird song . . .
the sniper paints his face
pale green

AI LI

accident site . . .
an umbrella
catching rain

A. A. MARCOFF

the way
the temple
alters the wind

PAMELA MILLER NESS

after all these years
ankle deep
in the other ocean

CHARLES TRUMBULL

October dusk
a plastic coffee lid
fills with rain

such innocent questions—sunflowers

we follow the fence
through knee-deep snowdrifts . . .
Pasternak's grave

FERRIS GILLI

ashes drifting
beyond charred fields
a hawk's slow curve

still no word
a kingfisher flies up
from dark water

ERNEST J. BERRY

contraction—
the darkness
between stars

mother's parasol
I unfold the dust
of other summers

storm clouds
the cry of a shearwater
circles the sky

CARL PATRICK

fireflies
my neighbor
has more

DAVID BURLEIGH

The morning paper—
I set down my coffee cup
in Buenos Aires

PAUL MULDOON

A hammock at dusk.
I scrimshaw a narwhal hunt
on a narwhal tusk.

Old burial ground.
That otherworldly scythe-swish
still the only sound.

CHARLES EASTER

close lightning
　the metallic taste
　　in my mouth

KEN JONES

Bone scan
the length
of a Brandenburg Concerto

These hills
have nothing to say
and go on saying it

AN'YA

one limb at a time
the falcon calls her fledglings
nearer to flight

ANNIE BACHINI

day after day
bits of a chained bicycle
disappear

MATT MORDEN

mountain wind
the stillness of a lamb
gathering crows

PAUL MACNEIL

paddle at rest
beads of water slide
from the loon's bill

the eider duck's dive
deeper
than his whiteness

RAFFAEL DE GRUTTOLA

lost in the lights
the high fly ball that
never comes down

PHILIP ROWLAND

under closed circuit
surveillance

old snow

on an island
in the pond

anchor
i
tic

a Bach fugue
hands separately
trying to make sense of
the rainy season

let
death
be

like
this
well

bucket
night
fall

inside an envelope
inside an envelope:
funeral money

DIMITAR ANAKIEV

spring evening—
the wheel of a troop carrier
crushes a lizard

JOHN CROOK

summer solstice—
the sun reaches a new place
on the fridge

high tide
oystercatchers follow
the curve of the bay

DOROTHY HOWARD

clear winter sky over the radio the first bombs

RANDY M. BROOKS

two lines in the water . . .
not a word between
father and son

all tongue
the clam in the fire's
hiss

razor wire
soldiers in the alley
tossing dice

BAN'YA NATSUISHI

From the future
a wind arrives
that blows the waterfall apart

JOHN J. DUNPHY

on a plaque
in the enemy's museum
names of our dead

JOHN MARTONE

new
robin
nest's

a
perfect
mud

circle
in

any-
day-now

honey
suckle

chimney swifts
at moments the sky
is empty

daughter waters father weeds their silence

forest skull's
sockets hold
my eyes

stand at
river

till you're
river's

standing
form

before
yellow

jacket's
sting
   fur's

touch

snow
on
moss

cu
mu
lus

STANFORD M. FORRESTER

summer afternoon . . .
losing the superball
on the first bounce

dog shit
or me
the fly doesn't care

they actually
are pretty quiet . . .
wild flowers

cold Aegean sun—
the temple
half stone, half shadow

RONALD BAATZ

look at the red throat
of the hummingbird—then tell
your story again

THOMAS A. CLARK

a terse note
repeated
farther in

ROBERTA BEARY

all day long
i feel its weight
the unworn necklace

third date—
the slow drift of the rowboat
in deep water

mother's day
a nurse unties
the restraints

thunder
the roses shift
into shadow

YVONNE HARDENBROOK

mountain hike
we drink from the beginning
of a great river

MATTHEW PAUL

lifting mist . . .
a flock of knots fans out
across the creek

teals whistle over the seawall long black freighters

my train delayed
by a suicide—
Easter drizzle

ALISON WILLIAMS

long evening—
a cloud's ragged edge
becomes rain

trying to switch on a light that already is late October

midday heat
a doll hung up to dry
by its hair

CONNIE DONLEYCOTT

crowd of umbrellas
a child opens his
face to the rain

lilt in her voice . . .
the moss-agate colors
in a sunlit wave

DAVID STEELE

stuck to the slab
the   i
of the frozen f sh

mending his fence
the neighbor's mouth
full of nails

MARK BROOKS

twilight shadows
the outline of a child
in sidewalk chalk

STANLEY PELTER

a pig's memory
it leads to colours
of hesitant hills

on tarmac
rooks smash snails
the harsh of rain

M. KETTNER

your hair drawn back
the sharp taste of radishes

gale force wind—
the shrieks of gulls
flying in place

STUART QUINE

moonlit the empty slot in the knife block

bolted and chained the way to the mountains

rain cairn crow

PAUL M.

back again—
the driftwood thrown
with all my strength

gathering clouds—
the creek's source
further up this valley

a line borrowed
from another poet
spring rain

unemployed
the uneven edge
of a quahog shell

deep winter
stars between the stars
I know

EMILY ROMANO

false dawn
the night watchman
relights his pipe

DAVE RUSSO

sun in the bones
of a darting minnow
my cell phone rings

JACK BARRY

passing headlights
snow gathers on
the horse's back

dead branch
finally falling
spring rain

entering Perseids
barred owl fledglings
beg to be fed

first evening cool
a preening goose
stretches one wing

snow light
not telling you
the whole dream

ALAN SUMMERS

down side streets—
gulls turning the sky
in and out

ROBERT MAJOR

silent Friends meeting . . .
the sound of chairs being moved
to enlarge the circle

BURNELL LIPPY

twenty below
the Milky Way
lined up with the river

geese
that stay—
winter rain

BILLIE WILSON

retreating glacier—
how long since we've heard
the black wolf's song

storm warnings—
the deep blue reach
of delphiniums

whalebone
from a beach near Savoonga—
winter rain

FAY AOYAGI

ants out of a hole—
when did I stop playing
the red toy piano?

monologue
of the deep sea fish
misty stars

intact zero fighter
at the Smithsonian—
cherry blossom rain

summer festival—
my Astro Boy mask
has lost its power

inside of me
a silkworm
spits out the night

icy rain
at the bottom of the lake
a door to yesterday

CAROLYN HALL

rain-streaked windows
    how to paint
    the finch's song

twilight
the poultry truck returns
with empty cages

windfall apples
what I think about
what I think

baiting one fish
with another
autumn dawn

so suddenly winter
baby teeth at the bottom
of the button jar

white wind the eyes of the dead seal missing

LENARD D. MOORE

late summer
black men spreading tar
on the side road

summer stars
the trumpet glinting
from its case

RAJIV LATHER

horizon
why and
why not

GABRIEL ROSENSTOCK

there must be light
where they come from—
chestnut blossoms

green green green
              the pines
                           seconds before snow

JON CONE

the cloud-edge on the horizon deer head in the freezer

ANDRÉ DUHAIME

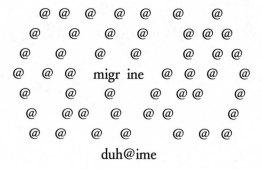

CURTIS DUNLAP

secluded highway—
in and out of my headlights
a John 3:16 sign

CHRISTOPHER PATCHEL

night train
we are all in this
alone

we turn turn our clocks ahead

PATRICK SWEENEY

Sparrows lift—
the stutterer's
sentence

Slow swing of willows through my own fault

under the nitrogen blue sky
the white horse
of my life

RICHARD GILBERT

a drowning man
pulled into violet worlds
grasping hydrangea

as an and you and you and you alone in the sea

YU CHANG

bearing down
on a borrowed pen
do not resuscitate

birdsong
my imaginary lover
alive again

PAUL PFLEUGER JR.

the heat
two boys take it
outside

where a bridge plank was the winter river

A darkness so deep
I am surrounded
by gold beetles

KAY F. ANDERSON

between a rock
and a hard place . . .
the oncologist's fish

Berlin Wall
a smooth stone
in my pocket

JOHN PHILLIPS

SNOW FALL IN FOG

hard
to
see
either

    through
    both

JACK GALMITZ

Under the pier
the sea roars in
A woman, a man

DIETMAR TAUCHNER

deep inside you no more war

spring longing
i follow animal tracks
as far as i can

gender god gone deep in the woods

new radio
the noise
of our origin

TIM SAMPSON

waiting out the storm—
a whole day spent
in a spider's life

ROBERT BAUER

chill wind—
the heart of an oak
leaves the chimney

EVE LUCKRING

behind the camera
I face
my family

centuries of whispers a cathedral beam collapses

in tune with
           its
            ob
            st
            ac
            l
            es
                  rain

SHAWN MCMURTAGH

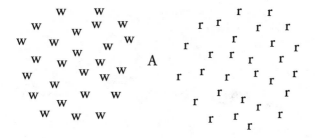

JÖRGEN JOHANSSON

scattered showers
a preschool class disappears
into the forest

a ladybird
b5 to c4

JOSEPH MASSEY

television light
lies on the
American lawn

MICHAEL MCCLURE

NOTH
ING
NESS
of
intelligence;
silver
sunlight
through
closed
eyelids

SONIA SANCHEZ

say no words
time is collapsing
in the woods

KARMA TENZING WANGCHUK

the fallen
and the falling leaves . . .
ten years of war

stone before stone buddha

waiting for me
to give it life—
my death poem

TOM PAINTING

big sky
the uncertain legs
of the foal

SCOTT METZ

a child's drawing
the ladder to the sun
only three steps

a
not
her
drop

&

it's
raining

meadow speaking the language she dreams in

the city's moan
phosphorescent
first snow

only american deaths count the stars

somewhere
fireflies are
eating rhinos

JOHN BARLOW

a dusting of snow light on the apple skins

down
the
leafless
beech
the
voice
of
a
nuthatch

the wind being farmed the wind that isn't

something startles
the rabbit field . . .
mackerel sky

somewhere
way beyond the grey . . .
the caw's crow

the piano hammers
barely moving . . .
night snow

MAX VERHART

out of the haze
the dog brings back
the wrong stick

GREG PIKO

galapagos
all the umbrellas proceed
at the same pace

D. CLAIRE GALLAGHER

a loon calls mosquitoes from nowhere

jet lag—
escalator teeth
from the nether world

MARSHALL HRYCIUK

pulling the shutters the braille of m/ y/ our desire

ALLAN BURNS

Kind of Blue the smell of rain

distant virga
the ranch dog's eyes
different colors

K-T boundary
on the sandstone bluff . . .
a rock wren calls

leaflight

coyote choir
we wake beneath
next season's stars

CHAD LEE ROBINSON

buffalo bones
a wind less than a whisper
in the summer grass

8 seconds . . .
the bull rider opens
a hand to the sky

migrating geese—
the things we thought we needed
darken the garage

full moon—
all our sounds
are vowels

one of the wolves
shows its face
firelight

RON C. MOSS

bloodwood moon
a starving dingo paces
the rain shadow

record heat
a soon-to-be mum
backs into a wave

starry night . . .
what's left of my life
is enough

JOHNNY BARANSKI

in the prison graveyard
just as he was in life—
convict 14302

TOM CLAUSEN

lunar eclipse—
back inside something I did
or didn't do

a rake in hand . . . the duck's mind

BILLY COLLINS

Innumerable
raindrops on the reservoir—
I stop to count some.

K. RAMESH

dawn . . .
the rooster for sacrifice
calls in the temple

ANN K. SCHWADER

razored through
to the void
raven

FRANCINE BANWARTH

sundogs
on the winter horizon . . .
another body count

the river freezes . . .
silence is also
an answer

LORIN FORD

on a bare twig rain beads what light there is

distant thunder
the future
in my bones

snake country the length of the shortcut

a dream time
before theirs and mine—
Wollemi Pine

JOHN SANDBACH

losing its name
a river
enters the sea

HARRIOT WEST

dusk
the girl we didn't like
with fireflies in her hair

SCOTT MASON

how deer
materialize
twilight

the passenger pigeon returns
on a canceled stamp

KALA RAMESH

deep in raga . . .
    sudden applause
startles the singer

ZINOVY VAYMAN

Yom Kippur Eve
by the church-turned-mosque
an ice cream truck's tune

CYRIL CHILDS

fog-filled harbour
someone somewhere drives
a nail through it

SUSAN CONSTABLE

rising river
a shadow still wedged
between the rocks

JEFF STILLMAN

sea returning for now I take it back

MARCUS LARSSON

autumn colours
we let mother lie
about our childhood

SANDRA SIMPSON

photos of her father
in enemy uniform—
the taste of almonds

facing a lily
the one-year-old
raises his fist

flirting
then denying—
cloud calligraphy

late summer rain
late summer rain
late summer rain

DARRELL LINDSEY

prey on the cave wall an arrow's unfinished flight

GEORGE DORSTY

low tide—
people seem
more honest

KWAME ALEXANDER

HAIKU

for miles & indigo

if your ancestors
could build pyramids then your
dreams are but mild stones

PETER NEWTON

standing in the middle of now here

the
animal
in
me
can't
be
spo
ken
to
tem
p
o
l
e

HELEN BUCKINGHAM

that point of white before christ muscles in

ALICE FRAMPTON

how many times
do I have to tell you
meteor shower

September morning . . .
sunlight in the impressions
of three thousand names

MARK HARRIS

        deep snow
               in a dream, I find
               her password in

burl bark grown into a wound a word

        heart
        wood
        her echo
        lalia

CLARE MCCOTTER

clouds in a mare's eye the fracture beyond repair

TYRONE MCDONALD

tunnel graffiti my brain is such a soft surface

GRAHAM NUNN

swinging the axe
sunlight splits
the firewood

MELISSA ALLEN

radiation leak moonlight on the fuel rods

nothing
I didn't know
before
maple
after
maple

JOHANNES S. H. BJERG

petrol moon
I play a bone flute
among sleeping dogs

SUSAN DIRIDONI

step back into the fragrance our histories mingling

vows jump their past-perfect membranes Eastertide

REBECCA LILLY

Daffodils
in our backyard—
we clown car it

Snow at dawn . . .
dead singers in their prime
on the radio

AN OVERVIEW OF
HAIKU IN ENGLISH

WHAT IS HAIKU?

A haiku is a kind of poem. It originated in Japan and is now written in more than fifty languages around the world. It evolved from an early collaborative linked form called *renga*, specifically from the opening verse of a renga, the *hokku*. *Hokku* were written as stand-alone poems by the sixteenth century, but it wasn't until the beginning of the twentieth century that the term *haiku* actually came into use.[1]

It was *hokku*, then, that English scholars and poets discovered at the end of the nineteenth century and tried to translate and write themselves. These short poems were baffling at first glance. They were shorter than virtually all Western poems, lacked Western metrics for the most part and rhyme altogether, and favored a content and sensibility that seemed alternately simplistic and enigmatic. They were traditionally written in a single vertical line of seventeen "syllables" (though what constitutes a syllable in Japanese differs from what constitutes one in English).[2] Vocal and poetic patterns in Japanese typically fall into phrases of five and seven sound-syllables, and are featured in all traditional Japanese verse forms—including haiku, which, as has become famously known, most often followed a 5-7-5 pattern.

This 5-7-5 pattern has served for a long time in popular culture as the defining characteristic of haiku. But there are other elements that are far more important to the way haiku work in English. One is the *kire*, or "cutting word," for instance, which results in juxtaposition between two images in the poem, guaranteeing that haiku are always about relationship, a stated or implied comparison of elements.

Another is a *kigo*, or "season word," a coded reference that works as a literary shortcut, connecting the poem at hand in the reader's mind with other poems on the same or similar topics. *Kigo* evoke not just other poems in the tradition but the look, feel, rhythm, and phenomena of the seasons, thereby condensing a fair bit of meaning as a kind of synecdoche, a useful technique in so short a poem. Other techniques, such as grammatically incomplete structure and asymmetrical phrase lengths, have often been adopted as well.

Haiku can range widely in terms of sensibility and tone. Over time, however, and especially following Matsuo Bashō's (1644–1694) example, certain elements have come to predominate: aesthetic principles such as *sabi* ("the desolation and beauty of loneliness; solitude, quiet"),[3] *wabi* ("a feeling of powerlessness; a sensation of great loneliness, or its cause"), [*mono no*] *aware* ("the deep feelings inherent in, or felt from, the world and experience of it"), *yūgen* ("mystery and depth"), and *karumi* ("lightness"). Still in other cases the poet seeks expressly to contradict these principles.

The "four pillars" of Japanese haiku—Bashō, Yosa Buson (1716–1783), Kobayashi Issa (1763–1828), and Masaoka Shiki (1867–1902), to whom may be added the poet-nun Chiyo-jo (1703–1775) and some twenty or thirty second-tier poets from the seventeenth to nineteenth centuries—have had an outsized influence on the development of haiku in the West, since their work has been, by far, the most translated into English and other Western languages. In recent years translations of more contemporary Japanese masters have been made available, and so we have come to appreciate poets such as Takahama Kyoshi (1874–1959), Kawahigashi Hekigodō (1873–1937), Osuga Otsuji (1881–1920), Taneda Santōka (1882–

1940), Ogiwara Seisensui (1884–1976), Ozaki Hōsai (1885–1926), Nakatsuka Ippekirō (1887–1946), and Kaneko Tohta (b. 1919) as masters of the genre.

THE ORIGINS OF HAIKU IN ENGLISH

Not surprisingly, the first haiku available in English were translations of Japanese originals. And the first students and writers of and about haiku were not poets but scholars, which conditioned our understanding of haiku for decades. William George Aston (1841–1911) was a pioneer in the Western study of Japanese literature. It's possible that the three *hokku* found in his *Grammar of the Japanese Written Language* (written in 1877) without ascription were written by him and are the first ever attempted in English.[4] Here's one of them:

FUJI CONCEALED IN A MIST.
Into a sea of mist whither hath Mt. Fuji sunk?

Whether the poems are originals or translations, we can be relatively certain they are the first of their kind to appear in English.

Even more influential was Aston's *History of Japanese Literature* (1899). This first major overview of

Japanese literature in English was the primary source of information about Japanese writing for poets such as Amy Lowell, Ezra Pound, and Kenneth Rexroth.

Two other early propagators of the genre are worth noting. Basil Hall Chamberlain (1850–1935) began translating Japanese verse as early as 1880. He notoriously equated haiku with the English epigram, and, seeking English equivalents, translated them into couplets.[5] Lafcadio Hearn (1850–1904) first published his translations in 1898 and showed a particular aptitude for the genre—some of his versions remain fresh even today. Here's one that is possibly the first English-language version of Bashō's famous *furuike ya*:

Old pond—frogs jumping in—sound of water.[6]

Many other translators tried their hand at the "new" poetry from Japan, with varying success. Compare here several translations, from a terse, "modern" conception to this fulsome and recklessly padded "romantic" version, of a famous Japanese original.[7]

natsugusa ya tsuwamono domo ga yame no ato
                                                    BASHŌ

Haply the summer grasses are
A relic of the warriors' dreams.

BASIL HALL CHAMBERLAIN

Asleep within the grave
The soldiers dream, and overhead
The summer grasses wave.

WILLIAM N. PORTER

Old battlefield, fresh with spring flowers again—
All that is left of the dream
Of twice ten thousand warriors slain.

CURTIS HIDDEN PAGE

The summer grass!
'Tis all that's left
Of ancient warriors' dreams.

INAZŌ NITOBE

THE FIRST HAIKU WRITTEN IN ENGLISH

Yone Noguchi (Noguchi Yonejirô, 1875–1947) wrote
the first haiku we can be certain was composed orig-
inally in English. His goal was to bring Japanese aes-
thetics and Zen to the West. Here's how he describes
that first attempt:

Although I was quite loyal to this seventeen sylla-ble form of Japanese poetry during many years of my foreign wandering, I had scarcely any moment to write a hokku in original Japanese or English, till the day when I most abruptly awoke in 1902 to the noise of Charing Cross where I wrote as follows:

Tell me the street to Heaven.
This? Or that? Oh, which?
What webs of streets![8]

Another early proponent of English-language haiku was Sadakichi Hartmann (1867–1944), a friend of Ezra Pound and almost certainly an influence on him. He offered work such as this:

White petals afloat
On a winding woodland stream—
What else is life's dream![9]

It was the Imagists, a group of poets in early twentieth-century Anglo-American poetry, who favored preci-sion of imagery and clear, sharp language. They took to haiku, not surprisingly, since most of their stated goals directly overlapped with elements to be found in it: the aspiration to perceive the thing directly, to express it without emotion or excess, concisely and in common language. None was more a collector (and disperser) of influences than Ezra Pound. In 1913 he published his famous "Metro" poem:

IN A STATION OF THE METRO
The apparition   of these faces   in the crowd :
Petals   on a wet, black bough .

Pound referred to this as a "hokku-like sentence."[10] This poem raises many questions that would be debated by practitioners of haiku in subsequent decades. Is it a three-line poem, or is it two lines with a title? Should haiku even have titles? Should they speak of contemporary topics, like subways, or must they be limited to "classical" content? Should their focus be contemporary and urban, as the first line here, or more austere and naturalistic, like the second? Or both? Is the allusion to Western mythology (here the story of Persephone) appropriate to the genre, or should haiku refer only to other haiku? Some of these issues have yet to be, and perhaps cannot be, settled definitively.

In addition to the most basic haiku techniques of juxtaposition and seasonality, some technical features of Pound's poem are quite farsighted as well. The two-line approach emphasizes the division between the two images. The unusual spacing of the lines slows the reader down. Even the punctuation is separated from the text, thus creating more space around the words, and a feeling not of a moment (the usual haiku time sense) but of some duration. The rhyme, if there can be said to be one, is simple vowel repetition, not a true masculine rhyme. These aspects all contribute to the ensemble effect—the integration of haiku sensibility into Western poetics, content, and techniques. It is, in fact, the first fully realized haiku in English.

Thus it is with this poem that our anthology commences.

THE FIRST WAVE

Pound merely dabbled in haiku, and we reproduce his three known examples. We chose to anthologize his final version of the "Metro" poem, while citing his first published version above, feeling his adjustments are instructive. He renders the first line in all-capitals, more clearly defining its role as the title. He eliminates the arbitrary, if suggestive, empty spaces, arriving at what becomes a more normative look and reading experience, perhaps feeling the poem was sufficient unto itself and therefore that it was unnecessary to draw undue attention to its scaffolding. He changed the colon terminating the second line to a semicolon, eliminating any feeling of causality or consequence the former symbol might impart.

Pound's two other examples are closer to what was to become the norm for English-language haiku (hereafter ELH)—three lines, short-long-short—though not to be employed slavishly ("Fan-Piece" is 5-7-7, and both it and "Ts'ai Chi'h" are seventeen words long). Both are more aligned with classical Japanese subject matter. They were products of the mid-1910s, after which Pound never revisited the genre, though his encounter with haiku certainly influenced techniques in the long work of his later career, most notably parts of the *Cantos*.

His work did, however, affect the activities of his fellow Imagists, who, buttressed by the teachings of Noguchi and Hartmann, prompted the first haiku craze in English. Newspapers held contests, and thousands of would-be poets made their first attempts at it, though nearly none of these results has been preserved.[11] Those that do remain are principally those of the Imagists themselves.

Amy Lowell was ELH's first champion, composing hundreds of such pieces and publishing entire books of them.[12] Some other poets in the Imagist tradition whose oeuvre features haiku include John Gould Fletcher and Yvor Winters.

As other major figures in American poetry became aware of haiku, they tried their hands at it. E. E. Cummings, whose most haikuesque work wouldn't appear for decades, published three "standard" (that is, 5-7-5) haiku in *The Harvard Monthly* in April of 1916. Charles Reznikoff wrote short poems that featured an acerbity and wit that *haikai* poetry in English had not possessed before, almost a repudiation of the sensibility of nature that had permeated the genre since its importation, although he also wrote poems based in nature. Langston Hughes brought an early African-American content to the genre, not only through his one clear example, but in other short lyrics which employed haiku techniques. Carl Sandburg (1878–1967) wrote short evocative lyrics, such as the following, which partake of the haiku flavor:

WINDOW

Night from a railroad car window
Is a great, dark, soft thing
Broken across with slashes of light.[13]

Wallace Stevens never termed anything he wrote haiku but was certainly aware of the genre. In 1917, during the first heyday of haiku in the United States, he published a quirky poem composed of thirteen short, imagistic stanzas. "Thirteen Ways of Looking at a Blackbird" became not only a signature early piece for the poet, but also remains unique in his oeuvre for those very characteristics that are most haikuesque. Consider the first stanza:

I
Among twenty snowy mountains,
The only moving thing
Was the eye of the blackbird.

Could this possibly be any more like a haiku? Untitled (except for the numeral), it is written in three lines with a division after the first line like a *kireji*, concerned with nature and our relationship with it, and notices, even among the majestic, the small and insignificant. Investing the commonplace with energy, it privileges life above all that majesty, insisting on our noticing just that. This is a clear instance of haiku sensibility. And although not all the stanzas are quite so "haiku normative," we might still consider "Thirteen Ways" to be the first haiku sequence in the language, a remarkable tour de force and a mature response to Pound's work. In half a decade, English haiku had produced its first two masterpieces.

William Carlos Williams (1883–1963), a doctor and poet, also adapted haiku to his own purposes, most notably in "The Red Wheelbarrow."[14] Much has been made of this poem as a lesson in perception and objectivism, but it is also suggestive of Williams' familiarity with haiku, which perhaps emboldened him to trust so entirely such a minimal statement of facts. Stripped of its first stanza ("so much depends / upon") we have

a red wheel
barrow

glazed with rain
water

beside the white
chickens.

which could be read as straight haiku, and a "seeing into things" cognate with the crossing of Western "realism" and Eastern technique. Other Williams poems, such as "Between Walls" and "The Locust Tree in Flower," further explore this relationship between content and technique that was a hallmark of his style.

The issue of which tradition—Japanese or Western —should predominate in English-language haiku persists. One early school of thought maintained that haiku is a poetic manifestation of Zen Buddhism and that what constitutes a great haiku is the revelation of *satori*, "intuitive awakening to the truth of experience rather than a conceptual understanding of its principles."[15] This position, not a prominent part of early scholarship and translation, blossomed for the first time in the work of Paul Reps, whose minimalist approach to the genre seems fresh even today and whose early combination of short imagistic poems and *sumi-e* (brush and ink) drawings constitutes the first body of *haiga* (haiku painting) in the West.

In the first wave of interest haiku had been taken up seriously and professionally by some of the best American poets, and from it they attempted to create something idiomatically English. It might have seemed haiku was on its way to becoming a recognized genre within the Western poetic canon—but it didn't happen. Haiku, after this initial flurry of activity, withered on the vine and was possibly head-ing toward extinction in English. There are many possible reasons: the lack of continuing interest among the best poets, the normalization of practice to its most overt characteristics (with lamentable results), suspicion of Japanese culture as that nation came to be perceived as an enemy of the West (culminating, of course, in the bombing at Pearl Harbor and World War II); or perhaps some combination of these and others. But after a promising start, haiku looked to be at a dead end a few decades after its birth in the West.

THE BEATS AND HAIKU

A few isolated events managed to keep haiku in English alive past the 1930s. The first was the publication of Asataro Miyamori's (1869–1952) *Anthology of Haiku, Ancient and Modern*, translations of Japanese originals that included, for the first time in the West, work of contemporary poets as well as the older masters. Of particular interest was Miyamori's addition of commentary, biographical information, and alternative translations, a model that would prove seminal in later translations.

More pertinently, Harold Gould Henderson (1890–1974), a professor of comparative literature at Columbia University, published the first serious study of Japanese haiku in English, *The Bamboo Broom*, in 1934. This book, from a scholar known and respected in the Western literary world, offered haiku a theoretical credibility in the same way that its adoption by Pound, Stevens, and others had given it a poetic basis. Henderson's authority continued throughout and beyond his lifetime, perhaps made most manifest in what he wrote in *Haiku in English* (1967): "What kind of poems [haiku] will eventually turn out to be will depend primarily on the poets who write them."[16] Obvious as this statement has come to seem, it gave permission to poets to take the genre into their own hands, even if they knew nothing, really, beyond available translations. We might well have arrived at this point anyway, but Henderson eased our way there by recognizing the problems inherent in mere imitation and urging poets to trust themselves and their language as they felt their way forward into the new territory.

Toward the end of the 1930s, however, events quite outside the ken of the haiku world conspired to bring interest in haiku, and much else, to a standstill. Japan's role in World War II changed its standing in the Western mind, and where once its cultural products were embraced for their novelty, they were now looked upon with distaste. It was a decade before they could again be considered in artistic, and not political, terms. And it took an outstanding and sympathetic approach to haiku to make it relevant to the West again. Reginald Horace Blyth (1898–1964) was tutor to the Crown Prince of Japan when the war broke out and was incarcerated for its duration. His four-volume study *Haiku* (1949–52), followed by his two-volume *History of Haiku* (1963–64), revolutionized the way Westerners perceived the genre. Blyth stated, "Haiku are to be understood from the Zen point of view,"[17] and his championing of what he felt was excellent in haiku, along with commentaries explaining why, had an effect on the practice of writing haiku that persists to this day. His work also made available to English readers for the first time thousands of poems that previously had not been known outside of Japan, broadening the scope of what haiku was seen to be. His influence reached beyond poets primarily interested in haiku and has been cited by devotees such as J. D. Salinger, Jack Kerouac, and Richard Wright.

Blyth's writings sparked a broad new activity in haiku, and, coupled with a postwar renaissance of interest in Eastern philosophy and religion, especially Zen, appealed in particular to the emerging

Beat generation. Figures prominent in popular culture such as Alan Watts, John Cage, and Daisetz Suzuki brought these "alternative" philosophical systems to the forefront of artistic thought, and Blyth's espousal of haiku and Zen made for a compelling combination that was much in keeping with the times.

Gary Snyder was introduced to haiku by Kenneth Rexroth, and in turn introduced it to Kerouac and Allen Ginsberg. His primary work was as a translator, especially from the Chinese, and as a poet with a keen feeling for natural environments. Haiku has been a minor part of his overall oeuvre. He nevertheless won the Masaoka Shiki International Haiku Grand Prize (2004) for his contribution to haiku, and many of his collections contain haiku or haiku-influenced poems. Ginsberg wrote not only haiku, but also a form he evolved from haiku called "American Sentences," seventeen grammatically complete syllables. The influence of haiku can be found in his longer work, though unlike some other poets, it made him hardly less voluble.

Jack Kerouac is one of the best chroniclers issuing from those times, and his *Dharma Bums* in particular, with its discussion directed toward haiku and Blyth's books, introduced many people to haiku when it was published in 1958. Kerouac adopted the genre as a principal means of expression throughout his life, and his collected haiku, or "pops," as he termed them, is one of the first great bodies of work in the genre outside Japan.[18]

He was also one of the first theoreticians of the genre in English. "The American Haiku is not exactly the Japanese Haiku," he wrote. "The Japanese Haiku is strictly disciplined to seventeen syllables but since the language structure is different I don't think American Haikus (short three-line poems intended to be completely packed with Void of Whole) should worry about syllables because American speech is something again . . . bursting to pop."[19]

Most important, the quality of Kerouac's haiku was consistently higher than anyone else's in the preceding thirty years. Even the best work published by his contemporaries fails to approach his variety, tone, energy, and understanding of what was essential to haiku. The quality and volume of the poems he produced makes the first sustained argument for haiku as art in English.

Several other Beat poets—Gregory Corso, Lew Welch, Jack Spicer, Lawrence Ferlinghetti, Albert Saijo, and Diane DiPrima—have offered their versions of haiku. Some are quite innovative, such as

Michael McClure's typographical blasts that some-what resemble Vorticist poems.

Another interesting figure who made his repu-tation as a novelist but spent considerable energy and thought coming to terms with haiku is Richard Wright. In the last four years of his life, while liv-ing in self-imposed exile in France, Wright wrote thousands of haiku, nearly all in a strict 5-7-5 for-mat and under the influence of Blyth's Zen-infused translations of the Japanese masters. He died before he had come to full maturity in the genre, but even so his handling of material, especially in his "mag-nolia" poems (a possible symbol of white culture),[20] suggests he was finding his way to true depth and resource within its strictures.

As the Beats were adopting the genre and bringing it unprecedented exposure, commercial publishers began to find a market for translations of Japanese haiku, nearly all of which took liberties with the originals. The Peter Pauper Press offered a series of attractively designed short collections in the 1950s, with translations by Peter Beilenson and (later) Harry Behn. These versions most commonly offered a 17-syllable count broken into four lines, the middle two indented, and all in small capitals, which fairly screamed at the reader. Harold Stewart's *A Net of*

Fireflies, which ran through nearly a hundred printings, offered rhymed couplets of iambic pentameter and took great license with the order of images. In contrast, translations of haiku and other genres by Geoffrey Bownas and Anthony Thwaite in *The Penguin Book of Japanese Verse* introduced Eastern poetry to thousands of readers in versions that were sharp and spare, in three lines and without "poetic" padding. Nevertheless, the standard for translation of haiku into English remained the versions of Blyth.

BEYOND THE BEATS

This proliferation of generally available publications had its impact: more and more poets were exposed to haiku in a variety of styles, and they began to find one another and for the first time to found organizations dedicated to haiku. In 1956 Helen Stiles Chenoweth founded the Writers Roundtable of Los Altos, California, which studied and wrote haiku. Their collection *Borrowed Water* (1966) was the first anthology of haiku written exclusively in English.

Another book that featured haiku became a surprise bestseller in 1964. Dag Hammarskjöld's *Markings*, translated by W. H. Auden and Leif Sjoberg, included nearly a hundred haiku by the late secretary-general of the United Nations. Although its popularity certainly owed much to the fame and story of its author, it also served as the first exposure to the genre for hundreds of thousands.

The previous year, the first journal dedicated to haiku outside Japan was founded in Platteville, Wisconsin. *American Haiku* was edited by James Bull and Don Eulert and then a cadre of early ELH poets in succession, including Clement Hoyt, Robert Spiess, Gustave Keyser, and Gary L. Brower, to mention only the most illustrious. The impact that *American Haiku* had on the growth of English-language haiku cannot be overstated.

Its first issue included poems by James W. Hackett, Larry Gates, O Mabson Southard, and Nick Virgilio, all of whom became exemplars of the nascent genre. *American Haiku* gave ELH poets writing haiku in English a place not only to publish their poems, but also to compare, for the first time, what was being attempted by others. Prior to *American Haiku* the bulk of haiku poets published, if at all, in newspapers and small journals and had almost no conversation with one another. With the founding of their own journal, Anglophone haiku poets at last had a way to chart their direction forward that responded to the input of contemporaries rather than imitation of the long-dead Japanese masters. Hackett's "Searching on the wind" was awarded first prize in the contest organized by the journal for the inaugural issue. Virgilio's "lily" and "bass" poems, two icons of the genre, were featured in the second.

With the arrival of *American Haiku*, some of the best of the early poets working in haiku became known to a larger public. James W. Hackett, the only contemporary non-Japanese haiku poet to have received the commendation of R. H. Blyth, set the early standard for evocativeness and drama. He experimented with form as well, and many of his best poems result from this exploration, but in the end remained most often committed to the traditional 5-7-5 formulation. His acute observations, especially of bird and insect behavior, elevated the level of expectation for nature-based poems in English.

At the same time Hackett was trying to fix the traditional format, Nick Virgilio was seeking to invent it anew. His innovations in form, content, and style resulted in some of the most identifiable poems in the genre, which retain their freshness to this day. Though he later became a bit more predictable in his handling of form, Virgilio was one of the first to gravitate toward a minimalist style, and his "weirds"—his term for poems strongly deviant from the norm (and particularly poems with run-together words) which he considered still to be within the haiku modality—are among the earliest wordplay haiku in our language.

O Mabson Southard is one of ELH's most distinctive stylists, employing a rare rococo finish to his unvarying traditional forms. His work, almost exclusively evocative nature haiku, is unmistakable in this context. Clement Hoyt, another strong advocate of traditional form, was more attracted to *senryū* (a related genre that focuses on the humorous and ironic activities of humankind) and wrote the first such volume in English.[21] Larry Gates made early experiments with the relationship between haiku and concrete poetry. And L. A. Davidson penned one of the most elusive and haunting haiku in the genre ("beyond") in a nearly unprecedented enigmatic style.

More journals followed, notably *Haiku Highlights* (founded by Jean Calkins, later edited by Lorraine Ellis Harr, who renamed it *Dragonfly*), *Haiku* (founded by Eric Amann, later edited by William J. Higginson), and *Haiku West* (founded by Leroy Kanterman). Each of these journals had its opinions regarding haiku and invited poets to contribute work that supported those positions. *Haiku*, for instance, was Zen-tinged, whereas *Haiku West* was traditional in its approach but also broader in its taste.

All these trajectories were gathered in what became the journal of record, *Modern Haiku* (founded by Kay Titus Mormino, subsequently edited by Robert Spiess, Lee Gurga, Charles Trumbull, and Paul Miller). Particularly beginning with the stewardship of Spiess, it became the flagship journal of the burgeoning haiku movement. Just about every ELH poet of note has appeared in its pages at one time or another.

Robert Spiess, known as "the gatekeeper" of English-language haiku, edited *American Haiku*, was poetry editor for *Modern Haiku* for some twenty-four years, and published nearly a dozen collections of his own haiku and two more of his epigrammatic "Speculations." In 2000 he received the Masaoka Shiki International Haiku Prize. His life was given over to poetry, and haiku specifically, and over the course of it he experimented with a wide variety of presentations, styles, and subjects within it. He was a mentor to a great many haiku poets and put his impress on the haiku world for more than four decades. His emphasis on theory as much as practice established a new level of understanding of haiku during his time.

John Wills is arguably the most important figure who emerged in haiku during the late 1960s and early 1970s. In contrast to the earlier *American*

Haiku model, his work argued for the stylistic revolution that has become the norm today: shorter, sharper, with a minimum of adjectives and an emphasis on action—there is seemingly always something moving in his poems. He experimented with presentation, portmanteau words (such as his iconic "troutswirl"), and, at the behest of his wife, Marlene (Wills) Mountain, sometimes employed the one-line format. Perhaps ELH's greatest nature poet, he deftly linked his observations to an emotional aura that made them feel larger than the natural situations he was rendering.

There were others as well. Virginia Brady Young, who studied poetry with Robert Frost, John Ciardi, Mark Van Doren, and others, abandoned her early traditionalist formulations in favor of an uncut minimalism that feels contemporary to our own day, though much at odds with her own. William J. Higginson, the most important scholar to emerge within the early movement, was also an innovative poet in his own right, championing "organic" form and recognizing the value of other non-English approaches to the genre before nearly anyone else. He undertook an in-depth and influential study of seasonality in haiku and had a particular love for its longer antecedent, *renga*. Anita Virgil's work approaches an "objectivist" modality, with striking images permitted to stand starkly as themselves to great effect. She also features powerful domestic and erotic elements in her work not found before her. She was one of the first to sustain a compelling vision throughout the course of an entire book, in particular *A 2nd Flake* and *One Potato Two Potato Etc.* Rod Willmot has one of the most diverse portfolios in haiku, having served as a leading critic, editor, publisher, and poet. His Burnt Lake Press was one of the first dedicated to haiku to produce books of comparable quality to those found in lyric poetry and other genres, and the important collections he published by Virgilio and Wills raised expectations about the level of excellence in haiku publishing.

Dedicated haiku journals led directly to the creation of organizations where poets could meet in person. It was perhaps inevitable that the area with the greatest concentration of such poets, New York City, would spawn the first formal organization dedicated to haiku outside Japan, the Haiku Society of America (founded by Harold G. Henderson and Leroy Kanterman in 1968). Central to its mission were regular meetings of poets to study, discuss, and write haiku. The society offered the first widely accepted definition of haiku (and other pertinent terms), later revised, and produced the important volume *A Haiku Path* (1994), which documents the process by which these definitions were formulated and presents much other material germane to the society's, and Western haiku's, history. The society also created its own journal, *Frogpond*, which vied with *Modern Haiku* for preeminence in the genre. The overlap of poets published in both was and remains considerable.

Other early groups include the Western World Haiku Society (founded by Lorraine Ellis Harr in 1972), the Yuki Teikei Haiku Society (founded by Kiyoko and Kiyoshi Tokutomi in 1975), and the North Carolina Haiku Society (founded by Rebecca Rust in 1979), the latter two of which still meet today.

Unsurprisingly, poets who came together in regional haiku societies became interested in how other such groups worked, and gatherings on a larger scale followed. The first such event in North America was hosted by Nick Virgilio in Philadelphia in 1971 and was as much a festival of Japanese arts as ELH. By the time of the second festival, organized by David Lloyd in Glassboro, New Jersey, attention had swung round primarily to haiku in English: the event was nothing less than a celebration of the publication of *The Haiku Anthology*, an event the host recognized to be of far-reaching consequences to poets in the West.

THE HAIKU ANTHOLOGY

Perhaps the most significant coming-of-age moment in the growth of haiku in the West was the publication, in 1974, of the first of three editions of *The Haiku Anthology*. Cor van den Heuvel, who had been writing haiku since the late 1950s and who had embraced the birth of the new journals dedicated to haiku in the 1960s, gathered a "representative selection" of published haiku in the mid-seventies, with the intention of showing that haiku, long dismissed in academic journals and mainstream publications, was now "becoming visible."[22]

With the publication of *The Haiku Anthology* by Anchor/Doubleday, ELH became fully fledged in the world of poetry. For the first time it was accessible to all interested parties, not just specialists. The influence of the volume cannot be overstated. Its readers came to recognize, many for the first time, that haiku was not simply a 5-7-5 nature sketch, but indeed a wide-ranging, emotive, capacious genre capable, in the right hands, of expressing anything a poet might wish to convey. It also put to an end, for the most part, the pervasive question (raised in Japan) of whether non-Japanese were capable of writing haiku. These poems were perhaps different from the ones found in the manifold volumes of classical translations, but they were just as compelling, just as deep, just as human.

At the same time, *The Haiku Anthology*'s editorial bent raised its own issues. The first volume, easily the slimmest of the three, was predictably a gleaning of the best haiku in English to be found, and not surprisingly the great bulk of these poems had been written by North American poets. By the second volume (1986) and especially the third (1999), however, interest and activity in the genre had moved far beyond North America, a change not reflected in these subsequent editions.

Nevertheless, the anthology provided the inestimable contribution of legitimizing the achievements of ELH poets. Even those previous volumes that had included some original English-language haiku, such as Yasuda's *A Pepper Pod*, were primarily books of translations. In *The Haiku Anthology* ELH displayed what it had achieved on its own, quite apart from Japanese originals or ethos and offered an argument for what was excellent, distinctive, and likely to last.

Several notable poets were featured in the first edition of the anthology. Gary Hotham offered a unique voice, an elusive canniness hard to limn, yet clearly felt. His long quiet devotion to quotidian themes makes his one of the most recognizable voices in the field. Michael McClintock, the *enfant terrible* of the genre in his early days, brought a young man's perspective to the art. His evocative poems based on his war experiences, as well as his erotic motifs, were as refreshing as they were shocking and opened new areas of content for examination. Alan Pizzarelli's matter-of-fact jocularity also offered a new note in a genre that had taken itself mostly seriously to this point. His work—a kind of rebuke to haiku—was in fact most often *senryū*. Elizabeth Searle Lamb's work is highlighted by Southwestern and exotic flavors and musical allusions, reflecting her various places of residence and professional life as a harpist.

Other poets who had more than a passing influence on the development of ELH who were featured in the first edition of the anthology included Foster Jewell, David Lloyd, Gerald Vizenor, and Larry Wiggin.

We should not overlook van den Heuvel's considerable contributions as a poet. His Americana subject matter (baseball, amusement parks, urban settings, and so on) and terse, prophetic form were original and trend-setting. He published a series of chapbooks under his own imprint (Chant Press) such as *sun in skull* (1961) and *the window-washer's pail* (1963) that have become classics in the field. And his range of tone, from sly to surreal, is unsurpassed in the early days of ELH.

Inspired, perhaps, by the success of *The Haiku Anthology*, a variety of new anthologies followed. The most significant of these were the *Third Coast Haiku Anthology* (1978), which introduced readers to the haiku of the Midwest, including such poets as Randy Brooks, Charlie Rossiter, and Ross Figgins, along with its editor Jeff Winke, and *Erotic Haiku* (1983), edited by Rod Willmot, which explored a topic rarely attempted in ELH before and featured work by many of the best-known poets of the day.

THE HAIKU COMMUNITY

With the proliferation of journals, organizations, and gatherings, English-language haiku had become a mature movement by the last couple of decades of the twentieth century. One of the consequences of this growth, however, was a divide in the perception of what ELH was: even as the genre was maturing beyond its early imitative phase, moving past most obvious notions of what was significant in haiku, and consequently coming into its own as literature, a more simplistic notion was emerging in popular culture. It identified the most overt characteristic of haiku—

that is, the syllable count—as the one irreducible element, and so for it the measure of haiku was its firmly fixed form. Readers only casually knowledgeable of the genre assumed the content of the poem could be anything an author might wish to express in seventeen syllables. On the other hand, the majority of poets who had studied the genre more closely had come to value a range of less obvious characteristics to a greater degree. The lack of equivalence between the English syllable and the Japanese *on* was widely accepted, and hence the argument for preserving the 5-7-5 syllable count was undermined. The characteristics poets considered "standard practice" included a three-line approach with short-long-short line lengths, the grouping of the first two lines against the third, or the last two against the first, an uneasy consensus on the usefulness of season words without any agreement that season words were equivalent to *kigo*, and a general concordance that standard poetic devices (assonance, alliteration, onomatopoeia, for instance) were acceptable in haiku with some incontrovertible exceptions (overt simile or metaphor, end rhyme).

This formulation of haiku was further codified by the publication of *The Haiku Handbook*, by William J. Higginson and Penny Harter, which specifically endorsed this ELH model as an approximation to "traditional form." Higginson carefully remarked that such a formulation should not be taken as the final word on the matter, but the persuasiveness of his arguments and the ubiquity of such examples to be found in the dedicated journals—and especially in the second revised edition of *The Haiku Anthology*—led many to adopt these practices as their primary form. It has proven remarkably durable and remains the most common format for literary haiku in English to be found today.

But of course anything posing as a standard is also a target, and there have been many writers who have taken exception to this neat formulation. In 1978, for instance, Haiku Canada was founded, and their leading poets brought a different approach to its haiku, exemplified through their most prominent publications (for example, *Haïku: Anthologie Canadienne / Canadian Anthology*, edited by Dorothy Howard and André Duhaime, was groundbreaking in its inclusivity as well as its bilinguality). The range of their journals ran from *Cicada* (founded in 1977 by Eric Amann) with its Zen approach all the way to *Inkstone* (founded in 1982 by Keith Southward and Marshall Hryciuk), which was decidedly anarcho-innovative. Dorothy Howard later continued the tradition of providing publication opportunities to haiku outliers in *Raw NerVZ* (founded in 1994). It featured work unlikely to find a home in the more normative journals, keeping alive in a public way the experimentalist tendencies of some of the best poets working in haiku at a time when ELH was becoming formulaic. It also incorporated a crotchety array of artwork that was well in keeping with the journal's ethos. The Canadian outlook was a refreshing challenge to what was becoming "community-think" and was quick to embrace unusual formats such as "eye-ku" (visual haiku), one-liners, typographical oddments, not to mention nonstandard content and style.

In the 1980s nearly a dozen journals came and went, chief among them *Dragonfly* (edited by Lorraine Ellis Harr), *High/Coo* (Randy Brooks), *Cicada* (now edited by William J. Higginson), and *Leanfrog* (Louis Cuneo). With more opportunities to publish due to the increases in the number of journals, a wider range of styles arose: the normative three-line season-word model was by far the predominant mode, but also one-line, two-line, four-line, and three-vertical-line formats, organic forms, eye-ku, concrete haiku, and much more. A full-scale investigation into the possibilities of the genre was underway as never before.

The second revised edition of *The Haiku Anthology* (1986) was every bit as important a milestone as the first had been. Where that first volume proved a modest and even tentative presentation, the second was altogether bolder in its insistence on the place haiku held in the literary world, and its breadth of poetic styles and content offered a compelling argument for the vitality of the genre. It featured not only generously expanded selections for the major figures of the first edition, but also the work of several newcomers who were to make a deep impression on future generations.

Martin Shea's is one of the most distinctive voices in the genre, focused on a dark and somewhat opaque reality that reveals its secrets grudgingly, either in the outer world or within the human heart and mind. His work is characterized by innovative layout, effective enjambment, and striking syntax and has been a major influence on younger haiku poets of two and three decades later.

Counterpoised to Shea might be Janice Bostok, whose more usual approach showcased a keen appreciation of nature and especially of birdlife, but also delivered some of the most poignant haiku of young motherhood ever penned. She not only introduced the genre to Australia (as well as New Zealand) but also founded its first dedicated journal (*Tweed*, 1972–79) and served as its editor as well as for the first *Australian Haiku Anthology* (2001).

If Bostok is godmother to Australian haiku, Marlene Mountain might be said to be the midwife of the American version. Mountain has been one of the most inventive, challenging, and controversial figures in the history of ELH. She was one of the first champions of the one-line format. In later years her insistence on non-normative haiku content, especially with political and social overtones, has made every haiku poet consider the relevance of their own work.

George Swede, a psychologist and professor, presented his inimical, keenly observed studies of human behavior in his poetry. Usually self-effacing and often comical, his poems have a sharp edge often not noticed at first reading. He has been a major anthologist of the Canadian and global haiku scene and also served as editor of *Frogpond*.

Alexis Rotella galvanized the haiku world with her "psychological haiku," poems primarily about the relationship between the sexes, most often cast in the first person. The sensuous and erotic quality of these poems were revolutionary and had a big impact on the immediate direction of haiku in the early 1980s. She also has had an abiding interest in *senryū* in general and is one of its best exponents in English.

Raymond Roseliep was a Catholic priest by vocation, and a poet by avocation. His lyrical and often humorous vignettes bespoke his interest in wider realms of poetry as well, and the vast preponderance of his work, nearly all of which is human-oriented, speaks of his preoccupation with human contact. He was one of haiku's greatest formal innovators, often a minimalist even by haiku standards, and he incorporated religious and philosophical themes into his work. His consistently high-quality work called up allusions from a variety of sources—other haiku and the world of culture at large.

Another poet with a philosophical bent, Robert Boldman wrote poems that looked and felt like no one else's. His minimalistic approach and eye for the telling image, leavened by a Zen-tinged spiritualism, resulted in poems that were seemingly obvious even at first reading but held uncanny depths. Some of his work presages the kind of effects later to be found in the work of the L=A=N=G=U=A=G=E poets. He vanished from the haiku scene in the late 1980s and has only recently reemerged (to a degree). Haiku scholar and poet Tom Lynch surmises, "Boldman has carried the poet's ego suffusion into nature about as far as it can be carried and still have him remain a poet, or still have a poem left to recount the experience. Beyond this level the poet and poetry, it would seem, are silent."[23]

Peggy Willis Lyles, one of our most notable haiku regionalists, is identified with domestic and nature themes. She wrote in a traditional style but was open to experimentation, especially later in her career. There is a decidedly Southern flavor to her oeuvre, drawing especially upon imagery from both Georgia and the low country around Charleston, South Carolina, where she was raised.

Ruth Yarrow brings her activist sensibility to bear in the preponderance of her haiku, apotheosizing the grandeur and subtlety of natural habitats, and infusing her poems with an ecological awareness. It is no easy feat to serve two masters in the space of such short poetry, but Yarrow's work is a convincing demonstration that it can be done. She also offers telling images of domestic scenes, among the finest ever captured.

Garry Gay is a professional photographer, and his trained eye is evident in his best work. A cofounder of Haiku North America, he is a master of *rengay*, a short linked form of his own devising. He has been seen primarily as a comic writer, and even his more serious work, which we have chosen to feature, usually contains touches of humor. He also writes with great economy (even for the genre) and often in an uncut mode—that is, without a natural break after either the second or third lines—which is not characteristic of many poets of his stature.

Other poets who gained notice from their appearance in the second version of the *Haiku Anthology* include Matsuo Allard, an early champion of the one-line form, and Jerry Kilbride, whose personal narrative flair is evident even in his shortest poems.

OTHER AMERICANS

Just as other Anglophone cultures have come to define haiku in ways more suitable to their bents, so too have haiku writers from America's minority communities.

Haiku in African-American culture has a lengthy tradition, having been first practiced by Lewis G. Alexander and Langston Hughes during the Harlem Renaissance of the 1920s in response to its prominence among the Imagists and other well-known mainstream American poets. It was taken up later by Robert Hayden, who was to become Consultant to the Library of Congress (the position we now call Poet Laureate of the United States) in 1976, and most famously by expatriate novelist Richard Wright. Wright first turned haiku toward an evocation of black culture, and there was no mistaking this direction in the hands of Etheridge Knight and Amiri Baraka. Civil rights activism, prison-yard blues, the urban experience, and jazz figured in their haiku and were adopted by later generations. Julius Lester suggests such themes in his work, as do Alice Walker and Rita Dove in their longer poems which adopt the haiku stanza form—that is, the traditional 5-7-5 syllabic array in three lines. Jazz, as a symbol of African-American contribution to culture as well as expressive voice, is a mainstay of the work of Lenard D. Moore and Kwame Alexander, among others, with Sonia Sanchez invoking blues in a similar manner.

Though less in the public eye, haiku has had an effect on Native American poetic practice as well. Haiku historian Charles Trumbull finds a number of interesting parallels between Native American poems and Japanese haiku,[24] including the manner in which they arrived in Anglophone culture, the manner in which each was willfully misinterpreted by its earliest champions, and the way the exotic elements of each has been exploited by the dominant culture. He finds poetic similarities between much Native American poetry and haiku in terms of concreteness, pattern, brevity, and aesthetics, as well as shared cultural elements such as a sympathetic relationship with nature, a felt quality of pathos leavened with humor, and an experience of displacement (especially for those Japanese who were interred in concentration camps during World War II).

Gerald Vizenor is easily the most prominent and accomplished Native American poet who has cultivated haiku as a means of personal expression. He came to the genre in the early 1960s and has continued to write haiku for the past five decades. His more than a dozen haiku books are concerned with Native American issues.

Other Native American poets who have incorporated haiku into their work include Kimberly Blæser, Raven Hail, Mary TallMountain, and Donna Beaver.

OUTLIERS

Haiku has also profited from the work of writers who have secured their primary reputations in other forms or even other genres. We have noted earlier the contributions of Pound and the Imagists; Stevens, Williams, Cummings, and other major mainstream American poets; and the Beats, in particular Kerouac. This interest in and contribution to the genre by mainstream poets has continued to the present. Although oftentimes their unfamiliarity with what has been done in the past half-century marks their work as outdated or heavy-handed, at times it is their very unfamiliarity with those developments that makes possible their unique contributions. Many of them came to haiku primarily from books of translations of Japanese poems or else personal experience with Japanese culture, including, for some, a period of their lives spent in Japan.

Cid Corman has had a long and complicated relationship with haiku, having translated many poems from the Japanese and having written with a sensibility that invites comparison to that of haiku. His journal *Origin* sometimes included translations of Japanese haiku, alongside Projectivist and Objectivist work, and he cotranslated *Oku no Hosomichi* (*Back Roads to Far Towns*) with Kamaike Susumu.

Ann Atwood married translations of Japanese haiku with her sumptuous and emotive nature photographs in a series of coffee table books that did much to spread the popularity of haiku in the 1960s and '70s. Her own haiku reinforced the refined, breathless style of art to which she aspired.

John Ashbery was impelled by Hiroaki Sato's one-line translations of haiku[25] to try his own hand at the genre. Idiosyncratic, powerful one-liners were the result. These poems have had an outsized influence on the course of later ELH and are especially important to the development of overlap between haiku and short-form poetry.

Patricia Donegan is a teacher, poet, meditator, and peace advocate. Her poems have a quiet center and a characteristic, unmistakeable Zen flavor.

John Martone is the mainstream poet with the greatest current influence on haiku, particularly in terms of form. His aerated, vertical line array bridges the gap between haiku and short poetry in the mode of William Carlos Williams and minimalists such as Corman, Robert Lax, and Frank Samperi. He advocates poetry as a way of life, following in the tradition endorsed by many—especially Japanese—haiku poets.

Whereas the preceding poets have made forays into haiku, Paul Muldoon has done the opposite, drawing haiku into his own sphere. His elliptical, allusive poems mirror the approach in his longer work, especially in their use of pastiche and quotation.

Billy Collins, who provided the introduction to this volume, has been an advocate of a stricter formal practice. Melded with his usual congenial surface, his poems offer a conversational and approachable body of work that is unique today.

Other outliers include John Tagliabue, who spent time in Japan and many of whose longer poems are imbued with haiku feeling; A. R. Ammons, whose early short lyrics closely approached haiku brevity and ethos; Larry Eigner, a poet early identified with "projective verse" but whose later work showed haiku's influence;[26] Richard Wilbur, who has adopted the "haiku stanza" (three lines of 5-7-5 English syllables) as a structural element in his recent poetry;[27] veteran surrealist Charles Henri Ford, said to have written a poem a day during the last several years of his life, and thus an advocate of the "haiku as life" school of thought; Tom Raworth, a British experimentalist whose haiku employ disjunctive syntax and a speedy, freely associational thought process; Seamus Heaney, a Nobel Prize winner who once compared the similarities of haiku and Old Irish verse and of the poetic mind in Japan and the United Kingdom;[28] and Robert Grenier, who wrote not haiku but text fragments that speak interestingly to the same concerns that haiku often address.

OTHER ENGLISHES

The success of *The Haiku Anthology*, with its focus on North American poets, gave rise to the idea that there was an "American style" of haiku, to be both admired and resisted. We have discussed earlier how some of the most prominent Canadians extended beyond the prevalent American standards. Here we consider some of the leading advocates of ELH in other Anglophone countries and even some in countries where English is not the first language.

The work of David Cobb is an excellent place to begin. The patriarch of British haiku, Cobb is its best-known exponent and cofounder (with Dee Evetts) of the British Haiku Society. He exhibits great range in his copious writings, which include many *senryū* and *haibun* (a combination of haiku and poetic prose) as well as haiku. He has a great fondness for humor and earthy content, which he handles with assurance and a lightness of touch.

His countrywoman Caroline Gourlay lives on the Welsh border, and the Black Hills inform much of her work, which is traditional and nature-oriented in the main but sometimes charged with a quite affecting human element. She displays a delicacy of style and a precision of language and shows flexibility in form, with occasional minimalist leanings.

Martin Lucas has been a leading exponent of British haiku, in friendly opposition to North American tendencies, for two decades. He founded and edited *Presence*, the most important haiku journal in English outside the United States, which reflects his naturalist bent coupled with a contemplative orientation. This quiet, musing approach is reflected in the best of his personal work as well.

John Barlow founded Snapshot Press, the most important ELH publishing house outside the United States. His work too is nature-based, closely observed, and tends toward the contemplative. With Lucas he edited the anthology *The New Haiku* (Snapshot Press, 2002). He has also coedited and published *Wing Beats*, an extensive anthology of avian-themed haiku.

Lorin Ford has emerged as the most important Australian haiku poet since Bostok. She evidences a broad stylistic range and is open to all currents, over which she demonstrates ample control. In addition to her own work she has made a considerable contribution through her online editing.

Dietmar Tauchner's first language is German. His writing exhibits much subtlety in English, even as it is marked by the circumstances of his geography. An Austrian, he is inspired to consider themes of myth, longing, and war. Of particular note is his Mauthausen sequence.[29] He is also the founder and past editor of the online German-English haiku journal *Chrysanthemum*.

Other poets included in this volume for whom English is not their first language are Dimitar Anakiev, Masaya Saito, Rajiv Lather, K. Ramesh, Kala Ramesh, Marcus Larsson, and Jörgen Johansson. In a very few instances we have selected work by poets who did not write in English at all but whose translated work has had a measurable impact on ELH. Dag Hammarskjöld, Günther Klinge, and Ban'ya Natsuishi fall into this category.

In addition, there is a goodly group of Anglophone expatriates who have spent time, or permanently settled, abroad. This has had a decided effect on some—James Kirkup's work, for example, is strongly marked by his experience of Japan in the post-atomic-bomb era. Others in this category include Patrick Sweeney, Michael Fessler, David Burleigh, Patricia Donegan, Richard Gilbert, and Paul Pfleuger Jr.

Philip Rowland, also an expatriate living in Japan and an editor of this volume, has a particular expertise in the boundaries between haiku and short-form poetry. His work is characterized by diverse experimental forms and ambiguous, modernist imagery. He is also founder and editor of the influential journal *NOON: journal of the short poem.*

THE GLOBALIZATION OF HAIKU

By the late twentieth century haiku had become integrated into nearly every poetic culture on the planet. Poets wishing to share their work needed to find a common language in which to do so. Few of these poets were fluent in Japanese, and for reasons more economic and political than poetic, the de facto international language of haiku became English.

The immediate consequence was that poets from all cultures began offering their poems in English as well as their vernacular tongue. Many of these early examples were not very accomplished, but over the past couple of decades the level of translation has improved remarkably.

This sharing of haiku around the world in a more or less agreed-upon common language was a new phenomenon, bolstered primarily by the advent of the Internet. The first electronic journal of haiku, *Dogwood Blossoms*, was founded by Gary Warner in 1993. From the beginning an international forum, it featured in its first year work from poets in Japan, Brazil, and the United States—all in English. The success of this project led in short order to other Internet haiku journals such as *Chaba* and *Agnieszka's Dowry*.

The founding, in 1994, of the Shiki Internet Haiku Salon, hosted by the Shiki Team, a group of poets based in Matsuyama, Japan, again attracted an international response in English. One of the elements of the salon, the *kukai*, was a thematic contest held each month that featured work by virtually every poet working in the genre. Additionally, the creation of the "Haiku in English" column by Kazuo Sato in the *Mainichi Daily News*, an English-language newspaper available throughout Japan, created an awareness of ELH as an international phenomenon.

In 1996 Red Moon Press began publishing its *Red Moon Anthology*, which culls the best ELH and related material as determined by eleven internationally esteemed poets from journals and books published around the world. This annual opportunity for recognition on a world stage encouraged poets not only to translate more of their work into English, but also to create English sections in their vernacular journals, especially in the Balkan nations, which adopted haiku in English with great enthusiasm.

Shortly thereafter (1996), William J. Higginson's international poetry almanac *Haiku World* brought more than six hundred poets together in the first world *saijiki*, a compendium of haiku organized by seasonality and topic. This vast enterprise mixed the various haiku cultures together in an unprecedented way and cultivated an appreciation of the differing values and standards that ran across these cultures. Poets from around the world now knew the names and work of other poets seining the same waters.

They desired to share their work more broadly, which was realized in the birth of global haiku conferences and organizations.

With the creation of Haiku North America (founded by Jerry Ball and Garry Gay and continued now by Gay, Michael Dylan Welch, and Paul Miller) in 1991, haiku gained a regular conference of the same professional quality as its best journals. This conference, held in different locales every two years, is the largest gathering of haiku poets in the world outside of Japan, regularly convening a hundred-plus participants to share presentations, readings, haiku-related and -inspired materials, and most of all, poems. Then, in 1996 and 1997, the Haiku International Association and the Haiku Society of America invited each other to reciprocal conferences, in Chicago and then Tokyo. The first openly international haiku conference had to wait until Tokyo, in 1999, hosting participants from France, Germany, and the United Kingdom. It was followed in 2000 by the Global Haiku Festival (Decatur, Illinois), the World Haiku Festival (London and Oxford, UK), and the World Haiku Association Inaugural Meeting (Tolmin, Slovenia). Each of these gatherings featured poets from at least three continents, and the main topic in each was the possibility of a world haiku. Of course, differences of opinion arose, but even so poets from around the world continued to write poems that sought a common ground and most often in English.

This widespread interest in global haiku did not preclude more local, regional, and national activities. The British Haiku Society, as mentioned, dates to 1989. HaikuOz has served as the base of operations for Australian haiku writers since 2000. And haiku poets in New Zealand, though without an organization of their own, have long been integrated into and accepted as part of the New Zealand Poetry Society. All these groups hold regular meetings, contests, and activities that keep their constituencies in contact.

The fact that ELH had become globalized did not alter the fact that it was based securely in North America. The Haiku North America 1999 conference included a celebration of the third revised edition of *The Haiku Anthology*. In this volume a third generation of ELH poets could be seen to be emerging.

One of these poets, Nick Avis, focuses primarily on nature and erotic themes, and he has produced some remarkable concrete poems. Though his output has been relatively small, he has maintained a high level of consistency throughout his career.

Wally Swist has adopted Thoreau as a model, and, following in the footsteps of Spiess and Wills, a lyrical evocation of the natural landscape is his primary mode. He has spent much time in the field, and his work displays a deep knowledge of the outdoors.

Dee Evetts, cofounder of the British Haiku Society with David Cobb, primarily writes poems based on human activity with a particular sensitivity to symbolic or gestural life. His work also reflects the multitude of places he has called home. He was born in the United Kingdom and has lived in Sweden, Thailand, Canada, and the United States. He is also an editor of the *New Resonance* series (Red Moon Press).

Lee Gurga has served as president of the Haiku Society of America, editor of *Modern Haiku*, and translator of contemporary Japanese haiku poets, alongside his work as poet. He tempers a kind of idyllic pastoral with an acerbic realism concerning the humans who occupy it. His recent work has taken a decidedly avant-garde turn.

Michael Dylan Welch is a champion of haiku on the Internet, and his current project, National Haiku Writing Month (NaHaWriMo), has inspired hundreds to try their hand at the genre. His own work features domestic themes and personae—his Neon Buddha poems are among his most celebrated—and a collection of parodies of other haiku poets, *Fig Newtons*, is his best-known book.

vincent tripi writes haiku inspired by wisdom literature and wildness, intimating a kinship he claims with Thoreau and other Transcendentalists. He's a devotee of the peripatetic lifestyle sometimes associated with haiku poets. His strong nature focus gave way to a more "spiritual" approach later, with the often playful quality in his work belying its serious philosophical undertones.

Christopher Herold discovered haiku in a Zen monastery in the 1960s, and his work has explored this dimension, in a primarily naturalistic setting, ever since. His haiku seek to amalgamate the traditional approach of Japanese haiku with the needs of the contemporary world. His handling of seasonality and his attunement to the music of language are worthy of particular notice.

Marian Olson was mentored by Elizabeth Searle Lamb and works with the same motifs—Southwestern nature and cultural themes—with a characteristic boldness of phrasing. Her haiku display an almost animistic vision as well as a profound sympathy for the fates of our fellow creatures, and an overall lyricism that relates her work to the longer genres she also writes.

Peter Yovu wrote more normative poems early on, but his later work has moved toward a challenging, experimental style, taking formal and technical risks that exemplify his public admonishment to other poets to "do something different."

Jim Kacian, the editor-in-chief of this volume, is one of the busiest people in haiku, having founded Red Moon Press, arguably the preeminent dedicated publishing house for ELH, and The Haiku Foundation, a nonprofit organization dedicated to preserving its rich tradition as well as creating new opportunities. He has written successfully in several modalities—psychological, traditional nature-based, humorous—and is identified with a variety of formats and techniques—one-line, organic, and process poems, especially those which invoke the passage of time, once considered outside haiku's province and hence a relative rarity. He is also well known as an editor, both of books (the *Red Moon Anthology* series, the *New Resonance* series, and others) and journals (*South by Southeast* and *Frogpond*).

Mike Dillon has worked in the genre for a couple of decades but has remained on the fringe of its activities. As a result, his voice is not as well known, but it possesses a quiet authority that makes his best work seem inevitable. He evokes the feel of a small-town sensibility without ever sacrificing a more worldly perspective.

John Stevenson, former president of the Haiku Society of America and editor of *Frogpond*, and presently managing editor of *The Heron's Nest*, is best known for his incisive, human-based haiku. He has a feeling for the unexpected but telling detail, often captured by misdirection in a third line that feels completely out of the blue yet exactly right.

Inevitably, some outstanding poets were omitted from all of the editions of *The Haiku Anthology*. In particular, there are three who merit special attention.

Paul O. Williams dates from the early *American Haiku* days but hit his stride in the 1980s. His work exhibits a strong naturalistic orientation and is on occasion extremely minimalistic. He was an English professor and noted science fiction writer and contributed to haiku theory and aesthetics, notably in his book of essays, *The Nick of Time*.

anne mckay was one of the most gifted lyricists ELH has ever known. Her work, judged to be iconoclastic through most of her life, certainly took liberties in terms of form and technique, often sprawling widely across a printed page. But she was a poet of the heart, primarily, and it is the emotive quality of her work that remains its principal strength today.

Charles B. Dickson came to haiku relatively late

in life, but his long-standing familiarity with the natural landscapes of his environment proved a fertile ground for his primarily traditional haiku, characterized by close observation and a strong sense of seasonality.

Much of the work of these and other top poets continued to appear in the small print journals well into the Internet era. Carrying the tradition forward, most of these journals showcase a particular aspect of haiku or else represent an organization. *Woodnotes* featured work by the Haiku Poets of Northern California. *Mayfly* focuses on the individual poem. *Hummingbird* melds haiku and short forms in a pleasing and educational mix. *South by Southeast* publishes international contemporary work but also includes appreciations of work by previous generations of ELH poets. *ant ant ant ant ant* explores the *gendai* (that is, contemporary, nonstandard Japanese) influence on Western haiku in intriguing, if irregularly produced, publications. *bottle rockets*, which offers higher than usual production values for a haiku specialty journal, features a notably broad range of styles, subjects, and approaches, while being the home of contemporary Zen-influenced haiku. *Acorn* favors high-quality traditional haiku, often with a strong orientation toward nature, in an uncluttered format.

Two journals in particular emerged as the necessary counterweights to *Modern Haiku* and *Frogpond*. The first of these was the aforementioned *Raw NerVZ* (1994–2005). At the other end of the spectrum, *The Heron's Nest* was the first electronic journal to achieve equal standing with the extant print journals. Founded by Christopher Herold and Alex Benedict in 1999, it sought to champion seasonal, traditional haiku in English, and quickly became the finest bastion of this sort of work to be found. Even more than *Modern Haiku* or *Frogpond*, the best of these haiku consistently could be found here. Whereas *Raw NerVZ* fed a cohort of poets who felt the need to explore the limits of haiku, *The Heron's Nest* satisfied those poets seeking the apotheoses of a kind of pure vision of what haiku in English might be. Both were needed to round out the possibilities required to keep haiku moving forward.

THE TWENTY-FIRST CENTURY

Beginning in 2004, Richard Gilbert serially published critical theory that was eventually to be titled "The Disjunctive Dragonfly" and incorporated into his seminal volume *Poems of Consciousness*.[30] In this essay, he argues that the conception of haiku we have inherited in the West is unduly narrow, not at all like that to be found in its native land, and that we would do well to broaden our expectations of what the genre might contain. In addition, he provides a set of tools we might use to create this enlarged haiku, terms not prescriptive but rather descriptive of the kinds of work already being done in haiku, however rarely, and which was difficult to discuss because of a lack of terminology. Although not all of Gilbert's suggested names have been adopted, serious conversation was inaugurated, and the result has been nothing short of a revolution in the kinds of haiku now regularly being published around the world. It is evident that this new valuation of achievement in haiku has been powerful and, even more, necessary.

The other significant tack that *Poems of Consciousness* takes is a study, with copious examples, of the *gendai* direction in Japanese haiku. *Gendai*, which simply means "modern," refers to the trend in Japanese haiku away from its most traditional practices— season words, syllable counts, and the like—over the past century. By providing poems, translations, and explanatory notes of the work of six leading *gendai* poets, Gilbert helped make this direction available to Western consideration, with considerable results.

Beyond this we can simply note that in the new

century there was more of everything that had already existed: more journals, more gatherings, more contests, more books, and many more poets feeling their way into the genre.

In the United Kingdom, Martin Lucas's *Presence* quickly became its most important journal, supplanting *Blithe Spirit* (the vehicle of the British Haiku Society), but it was not alone. ai li's short-lived but elegant and atmospheric *Still* had an enthusiastic following, as did Jim Norton's *Haiku Spirit*, out of Ireland. And *The Haiku Calendar* (from Snapshot Press) has long been a favorite place for ELH poets to appear.

Down Under there was activity as well. For years the general literary journals *Free XpresSions* and *The Famous Reporter* offered regular haiku columns. Dedicated haiku journals such as *Yellow Moon* and *Spin* appeared later. And in New Zealand *Kokako*, a beautiful and simple biannual, specializes in kiwi haiku.

In addition, there was an even more marked abundance of haiku participation on the Internet. *Haijinx* featured the playful side of haiku; *Simply Haiku* offered a broad perspective, including commentary and theory. More recently, *Tinywords*, *Notes from the Gean*, *Shamrock Haiku Journal*, and *A Hundred Gourds* have offered readers consistently high-quality content. Even in countries where English was not the primary language one could find English-language online journals, such as *Temps Libres* (English and French), and *Whirligig* (English, Dutch, and "guest languages").

In the years since the third edition of *The Haiku Anthology*, other poets have naturally emerged as leaders in the field. Many of these arose through their work online, although some have taken a more traditional route. Stanford M. Forrester's unique sense of humor, coupled with a Buddhist sensibility, marks his oeuvre in a very distinctive way. Although much of his work exhibits a light touch, he can convey a significant gravity when he chooses. His later poems, in particular, demonstrate considerable nuance in handling weighty themes. As previously mentioned, he founded *bottle rockets* and has been its editor for more than a decade.

Paul Miller, writing as paul m., works in both nature-oriented and psychological modes, one of the few who straddles the divide comfortably and successfully. His style is equally diverse, poised between traditional and experimental modes of presentation. He became the editor of *Modern Haiku* in 2013.

Fay Aoyagi was born in Japan but has lived much of her adult life in the United States. Her work has opened haiku to increasingly subjective, mythic, and whimsical modes of expression and content. Paradoxically, these challenging new modalities are offered in traditional dress, for the most part, including her handling of form and seasonality.

Cherie Hunter Day's professional science background enhances her approach to nature themes, and her time in the field is much in evidence. Her recent work exhibits a serious consideration of the more experimental trends to be found in the genre.

Chris Gordon has created an interesting dialogue between contemporary Japanese and English-language practices with the creation of his eclectic journal *ant ant ant ant ant* as well as with his own work. Each involves original subject matter couched either in the most traditional of garb (fine papers, 5-7-5 format), or the most avant-garde (irregular appearance, run-on uncut one-liners). Yet his primary theme is relationship, and his work remains, for all its challenges, accessible.

Scott Metz is challenging normative haiku on every level, as a poet with his explorations into found haiku, striking wordplay, typography, and surreal content, but also as an editor and anthologist. His online journal *Roadrunner* is the flagship of the experimentalist cadre of contemporary poets, and his anthology *Haiku 21* (coedited by Lee Gurga) is an inspiring argument for what's best in today's haiku.

In 1999 Red Moon Press began publishing the

New Resonance series, which showcases emerging talent in English-language haiku. Many poets featured in these biennial volumes are now among the most honored poets of contemporary ELH. These include the already-mentioned Lorin Ford, Gordon, Metz, Miller, Pfleuger Jr., and Tauchner, and the several that follow.

Roberta Beary has found her inspiration primarily in relationships in families and between the sexes, and in human rights. She has contributed significantly to the growth of haibun as well. Her book *The Unworn Necklace* was awarded a William Carlos Williams Award Honorable Mention by the Poetry Society of America in 2007, the first such honor for a book of haiku.

Carolyn Hall has received a string of accolades and prizes for her work, which exemplifies the finest tendencies of traditional style. Her later publications, though, suggest she is increasingly open to experimentation. She edited the journal *Acorn* from 2008 to 2012, and both expanded and improved the layout of the journal.

William Ramsey's work in haiku is completely idiosyncratic, interweaving overtly philosophical themes with a religious underpinning in search of a "sacramental" feeling. The consequence is a meditative poesy that springs from concrete images to emotive states in a very brief compass, which aligns him with the more experimental elements in haiku.

Jack Barry's self-sufficiency (he has lived for many years in a treehouse he built himself) has inspired the subject matter of much of his poetry. Unsurprisingly, his is a strongly traditional voice, centered in nature and environmental awareness but not without psychological resonance and a self-effacing humor.

Chad Lee Robinson takes much of his inspiration from his geographical situation: a lifelong resident of South Dakota, he fashions himself as a poet of small towns and the Great Plains. The result is a normative but contemporary style that often poignantly engages themes of life and death.

Allan Burns, an editor of this volume, seeks the naturalist's path as his way in haiku. His expertise in ornithology and environmental issues informs many of his best poems, which feature an updated traditional structure and feel. His comparative haiku series *Montage* was published as a thematic anthology by The Haiku Foundation in 2010.

THE NEXT HUNDRED YEARS

From the beginning, haiku in English has faced certain challenges that have marginalized its adoption, practice, and impact in the English literary tradition. The perception that haiku could not be truly written by a non-Japanese, an attitude maintained even today by some conservative *haijin* in Japan, brought into question the entire enterprise. The fact that the genre became available to Western readers at a time when it was undergoing an uncharacteristic period of conservatism in Japan limited the range of possibilities that poets saw in the new form. It has entered maturity in the West at a time when the pastoral, in which tradition haiku certainly must be viewed, is deeply unfashionable. It has been presented, especially since the 1950s (that is, throughout the time of its entire mature adoption in the West), as a kind of wisdom literature, which rarely attracts serious poetical, scholarly, or critical attention. It has been taken up largely outside the officially sanctioned domain of "serious poetry" by ordinary people and thus has been seen as a hobby rather than a worthy artistic pursuit. It has been burdened by the proliferation of thousands of uninspired, yet published, examples that reinforce the negative stereotypes to which haiku has been subjected. And it has been unwilling in the main to engage in serious critical discussion of its poems published in its journals and books, opting instead for an amiability that has encouraged a clubby atmosphere.

Nevertheless, English-language haiku has met each of these impediments with its own specific response, and while the consequences of these responses have been mixed, it has managed to maintain an upward curve, both in terms of popularity and achievement. More people than ever are trying their hand at haiku, and the word itself has a cultural aura that links it with the avant-garde. More important, an increasing number of its best poets are exploring ways in which to keep haiku not merely in contact with its traditional roots, but equally relevant to its current circumstances.

The majority of the poets in the final quarter of this anthology are represented by a single poem. They have come to maturity in the genre only in the last few years, and their mark upon haiku has yet to be fully revealed. But it is instructive to see that most of them have opted to look for additional means of expression within the haiku tradition. This is not a rejection of the tradition but, rather, an expansion of it, a discovery of techniques appropriate to the poems that poets are using to meet their needs. Not all poems will require these techniques—one-line poems, organic form, untrustworthy narrators, and the like—and not all poets will choose them, but they have at least become available within the realm of haiku without seeming too ostentatious or too self-dramatizing. The number of tools at our disposal grows.

The biggest challenge haiku faces from within is finding the right balance between remaining true to its roots and accommodating contemporary life so as to remain vital. For decades conservative elements in Japanese haiku sought to exclude modern objects such as automobiles, penicillin, and radiation, because such things were not mentioned in classical haiku. That attitude was taken up to a certain degree by the first imitators of Japanese haiku in the West and still attaches to ELH today. But such practice simply renders haiku an anachronism, incapable of responding to present conditions. One heartening sign that things are changing is the recent online haiku movement "We Are All Japan." Poets from around the world responded to the tsunami that struck Japan in 2011 with empathy and solidarity. Of course, a tsunami is a natural event and as such a permissible topic by even the most conservative interpretations of classical haiku. But the most immediate danger following the receding of the water was the meltdown of the nuclear power plant in Fukushima, and this human-created threat was the content of the preponderance of poems.

The ability to respond to such a contemporary reality within the scope of such a classical genre gave these poets more than a voyeur's connection with the events. One may quarrel over whether or not the sentiments of these poems are on target, but it's impossible to naysay the possibility of haiku functioning as a tool to permit such a sentiment to be expressed.

On a theoretical level a great deal of the consternation felt by poets relates to the growth pangs of the genre as it moves beyond its pastoral roots and embraces a more complete modernity. Pastoral emphasizes, among other things, a recognition that the complexity of the world is mastered in the simplicity of the life lived close to the land. This is an increasingly difficult position to defend, since in a world of combat drones, GPS's, and the World Wide Web, that kind of removal from society is rare indeed. It's true that such messages as the pastoral may impart still hold power in our social conversation. However, these messages are more mediated than before: even the most remote hermit will hear jets fly above his hovel, and the water he takes from the stream may well be contaminated by mining upstream or at least tamed by a dam that protects him from floods.

At the same time, the subject of the best poetry

has always been the wild—that over which we have little or no control—whatever "wild" might mean in a particular culture. Haiku poets continue to approach the "wild" not only in their most modernistic work, but in their most traditional. Haiku is one of very few resources we have for combating anthropocentric thought and environmental disregard. The nature emphasis found in traditional haiku takes on new meaning in our contemporary context. A deliberate and sophisticated direction of attention in contemporary haiku toward naturalistic objects doesn't just conserve tradition; it also consciously challenges anthropocentric creep and promotes needed consciousness of what's outside the ever-sprawling human hive in this age of habitat destruction, species extinction, pollution, overpopulation, and global warming, not to mention our modern alienation from nature. We sense this layer of intention in the work of the most sophisticated naturalistic practitioners. As such poetry aligns with the progressive environmental movement, its traditional elements actually read as avant-garde, in its literal sense.

Perhaps we can find reconciliation of these concerns, and our way forward in haiku, in the spirit of one of its great exemplars. Bashō wrote, "Do not seek to follow in the footsteps of the masters. Seek what they sought." It is the cultivation of this spirit that will most ensure that haiku continues as a living poetic genre.

The best poets working in haiku are responsive to the conditional aspects of reality, and their work is reflective of this awareness, in terms of form as well as content. The challenge, as always, is neither to innovate for innovation's sake, nor to constrain for tradition's sake, but to find exactly the right form, the right phrase, the right context, to express contemporary reality. So long as haiku remains responsive to these changing conditions, it will change and, in so doing, remain vital.

Jim Kacian

NOTES

1. An excellent treatment of this history can be found in Hiroaki Sato's *One Hundred Frogs: From Renga to Haiku to English* (New York: Weatherhill, 1983).
2. See Richard Gilbert, "Stalking the Wild Onji," in *Poems of Consciousness: Contemporary Japanese & English-language Haiku in Cross-cultural Perspective* (Winchester, Va.: Red Moon Press, 2008) for a detailed consideration of this topic.
3. All definitions quoted from *The Princeton Companion to*

Classical Japanese Literature, edited by Earl Miner, Hiroko Odagiri, and Robert E. Morrell (Princeton, N.J.: Princeton University Press, 1985).

4. Charles Trumbull, "Research Note: W. G. Aston," *Modern Haiku* 39.3 (2008): 59–63.

5. See Basil Hall Chamberlain, "Bashō and the Japanese Poetical Epigram," *Transactions of the Asiatic Society of Japan* 2:30 (1902).

6. Lafcadio Hearn, *Japanese Lyrics* (Boston: Houghton Mifflin, 1915).

7. All quoted in Asataro Miyamori, *An Anthology of Haiku, Ancient and Modern* (Tokyo: Chugai Printing Co., 1932).

8. Yone Noguchi, *Through the Torii* (Boston: Four Seas Company, 1914).

9. Sadakichi Hartmann, *Tanka and Haikai: Japanese Rhythms* (San Francisco, 1916).

10. Ezra Pound, "Vorticism," *The Fortnightly Review* 571 (September 1, 1914): 465–67.

11. An exception would be R. Crawford's winning entry, along with thirteen other haiku and two sequences in the reporting of the Sydney *Bulletin*'s *haikai* contest, August 12, 1899, held in response to the publication of W. G. Aston's *History of Japanese Literature*. The prize was 10s. 6d., about a day's wage.

12. For example, Amy Lowell, *Pictures of the Floating World* (Boston: Houghton Mifflin, 1919).

13. Carl Sandburg, *Chicago Poems* (New York: Henry Holt and Company, 1916).

14. William Carlos Williams, *Spring and All* (New York: Contact Publishing Co., 1923).

15. Miner, op. cit.

16. Harold Henderson (New York: Japan Society, 1967), p. 13.

17. R. H. Blyth, *Haiku*, vol. I (Tokyo: Hokuseido, 1949), p. 5.

18. Jack Kerouac, *The Book of Haikus* (New York: Penguin, 2003).

19. Jack Kerouac, *American Haikus* (Montclair, N.J.: Caliban Press, 1986).

20. Suggested by Michael Dylan Welch in his unpublished draft "We Are Still Not Free: Color in Richard Wright's *This Other World*," p. 13.

21. Clement Hoyt, *County Seat* (Platteville, Wis.: American Haiku Press, 1966).

22. Cor van den Heuvel, ed., *The Haiku Anthology: English Language Haiku by Contemporary American and Canadian Poets* (Garden City, N.Y.: Doubleday Anchor Books, 1974), p. xxxiv.

23. Tom Lynch, "Intersecting Influences in American Haiku," in *Modernity in East-West Literary Criticism: New Readings*, edited by Yoshinobu Hakutani (Madison, N.J.: Fairleigh Dickinson University Press; London; Cranbury, N.J.: Associated University Presses, 2001): 131.

24. Charles Trumbull, "The Uses of Haiku: Native American Writers," draft presented at the Seabeck Haiku Conference, September 2010.

25. *From the Country of Eight Islands*, edited and translated by Hiroaki Sato and Burton Watson (New York: Columbia University Press, 1981).

26. As in Larry Eigner, *Air in the Trees* (Santa Rosa, Calif.: Black Sparrow Press, 1968).

27. See for instance Richard Wilbur, *ANTEROOMS: New Poems and Translations* (New York: Houghton Mifflin Harcourt, 2011).

28. Seamus Heaney, *Our Shared Japan* (Dublin: Dedalus Press, 2007).

29. Mauthausen, a small market town in Austria, was the site of the Mauthausen-Gusen concentration camp complex during World War II.

30. Gilbert, op. cit.

INDEX OF POETS AND CREDITS

ABBREVIATIONS

U.S. Publications: *AC*: *Acorn*; *AH*: *American Haiku*; *ANT*: *AntAnt-AntAntAnt*; *BR*: *bottle rockets*; *BS*: *Brussels Sprout*; *CI*: *Cicada*; *DH*: Cornell University Mann Library *Daily Haiku*; *DR*: *Dragonfly*; *EPN*: *Electronic Poetry Network*; *FP*: *Frogpond* (International Journal of the Haiku Society of America); *GEP*: *Geppo Journal for Haiku Study*; *HH*: *Haiku Headlines*; *HI*: *Haiku Highlights*; *HM*: *Haiku Magazine*; *HW*: *Haiku West*; *THN*: *The Heron's Nest*; *HUM*: *Hummingbird*; *MP*: *Mariposa*; *MF*: *Mayfly*; *MH*: *Modern Haiku*; *PN*: *Penumbra*; *PER*: *Persimmon*; *PO*: *Poetry*; *PJ*: *Prune Juice*; *RR*: *Roadrunner*; *SO*: *Seer Ox*; *SSE*: *South by Southeast*; *SF*: *Starfish*; *UDS*: *Upstate Dim Sum*; *WC*: *Wind Chimes*; *WN*: *Woodnotes*.

Other Publications: *BS*: *Blithe Spirit* (Journal of the British Haiku Society); *CH*: *Chrysanthemum* (Austria); *HCal*: *The Haiku Calendar* (UK); *HCR*: *Haiku Canada Newsletter/Review*; *HP*: *Haiku Presence* (later simply *Presence*, UK); *MDN*: *Mainichi Daily News* (Japan); *NC*: *New Cicada* (Japan); *NO*: *NOON: Journal of the Short Poem* (Japan); *NG*: *Notes from the Gean* (Scotland); *PW*: *Paper Wasp* (Australia); *RN*: *Raw NerVZ* (Canada); *SHM*: *Shamrock: Journal of the Irish Haiku Society*; *SHI*: *Shiki Internet Kukai* (Japan); *SN*: *Snapshots* (UK).

Contests: GB: Gerald R. Brady Senryu Contest (Haiku Society of America); HNA: Haiku North America Haiku Contest; HPNC: Haiku Poets of Northern California Haiku Contest; HNH: HaikuNow! International Haiku Contest (the Haiku Foundation); HGH: Harold G. Henderson Haiku Contest (Haiku Society of America); JAL: Japan Airlines Contest; KU: Kusamakura University International Haiku Competition; PEN: National League of American Pen Women Haiku Contest; SP: Robert Spiess Memorial Haiku Competition (*Modern Haiku*); WPA: Francine Porad Haiku Contest (Washington Poets Association); WW: *With Words* International Online Haiku Competition.

Presses (*italicized if defunct*): AHA: AHA Books (Gualala CA); BLP: *Burnt Lake Press* (Sherbrooke QC); BMP: *Black Moss Press* (Windsor ONT); BRP: bottle rockets press (Wethersfield CT); BB: Brooks Books (Decatur IL); CET: Charles E. Tuttle Publishing (Rutland VT and Tokyo); DNP: Deep North Press (Evanston IL); FH: *From Here Books* (Paterson NJ and Santa Fe NM); HSA: HSA Annual Member Anthologies (various locations); HB: Harcourt, Brace & World (New York); HR: Harper & Row (New York); HCP: *High/Coo Press* (Battle Ground IN); IP: Iron Press (South Shields UK); KP: Katsura Press (Portland OR); KR: King's Road Press (Pointe Claire QC); LAP: La Alameda Press (Albuquerque NM); MHP: Modern Haiku Press (Lincoln IL); WWN: W. W. Norton (New York); PP: *Post Pressed* (Flaxton QLD Australia); PH: Press Here Books (Foster City CA and Sammamish WA); PR: *Proof Press* (Aylmer QC); RMP: Red Moon Press (Winchester VA); SAK: *Saki Press* (Normal IL); SW: *Smythe-Waithe Press* (San Francisco); SNP: Snapshot Press (Liverpool UK); SSA: Spring Street Anthology (New York); SWP: Swamp Press (Northfield MA); TP: Tribe Press (Greenfield MA); WCP: *Wind Chimes Press* (Glen Burnie MD).

Bibliographies where offered list only major volumes and/or volumes from which poems have been selected.

Addiss, Stephen (b. 2 April 1935 New York NY, r. Midlothian VA) Credits: "facing a lily" *PJ* 2 (2009); "flirting" *MH* 41:3 (2010); "late summer rain" *Cloud Calligraphy.* Bibliography: *Cloud Calligraphy* (RMP 2010). Permission: from the author. **p. 288.**

ai li (b. 20 October 19xx Malaya, r. London UK) Credits: "accident site" *MH* 29:1 (1998). Permission: from the author. **p. 176.**

Alexander, Kwame (21 August 1968 New York NY, r. Fairfax VA) Credits: "Haiku" *Just Us: poems and counterpoems* (Black Words Press, Fairfax VA 1995). Permission: from the author. **p. 291.**

Allard, Matsuo (b. 15 December 1949 Manchester NH, r. Manchester NH) Credits: "alone at 3:00 a.m." and "higher this time" *Bird Day Afternoon*; "an icicle" *Cicada* 3:2 (1979); "deep in my notebook" *Cicada* 5:1 (1981). Bibliography: *Bird Day Afternoon* (HCP 1978). Permission: no known literary executor. **p. 80.**

Allen, Melissa (b. 6 February 1969 Torrington CT, r. Madison WI) Credits: "nothing" *Notes from the Gean* 3:2 (2011); "radiation leak" *Haijinx* IV:1 (2011). Permission: from the author. **p. 300.**

Ammons, A. R. (b. 18 February 1926 Whiteville NC, d. 25 February 2001 Ithaca NY) Credits: "Small Song" *Northfield Poems.* Bibliography: *Northfield Poems* (Cornell University Press 1966); *The Really Short Poems of A. R. Ammons* (WWN 1990). Permission: "Small Song". Copyright © 1969 by A. R. Ammons, from *Collected Poems 1951–1971* by A. R. Ammons. Used by permission of W. W. Norton & Company, Inc. **p. 32.**

Anakiev, Dimitar (b. 15 April 1960 Belgrade Yugoslavia, r. Radovljica Slovenia) Credits: "spring evening" *Knots.* Bibliography: (editor) *Knots: The Anthology of Southeastern Europe Haiku Poetry* (Prijatelj Press 1999); *rustic* (RMP 2010). Permission: from the author. **p. 194.**

Anderson, Kay F. (b. 29 July 1934 Moline IL, d. 8 February 2007 Redwood City CA) Credits: "between a rock" *THN* 6:9 (2004). Bibliography: *Third Morning: a posthumous collection of the haiku of Kay F. Anderson* (RMP 2008). Permission: from the estate of the author. **p. 243.**

an'ya (b. 2 September 1947 Long Beach CA, r. Westfir OR) Credits: "one limb at a time" *THN* 1.2 (1999). Bibliography: *Haiku for a Moonless Night* vol. I (Natal*Light Press 2003). Permission: from the author. **p. 187.**

Aoyagi, Fay (b. 1956 Japan, r. San Francisco CA) Credits: "ants out of a hole" *RR* VI:3 (2006); "icy rain" *DH* (7 March 2008); "inside of me" *Beyond the Reach of My Chopsticks*; "intact zero fighter" *Chrysanthemum Love*; "monologue" *MH* 33:3 (2002); "summer festival" *MP* 10 (2004). Bibliography: *Chrysanthemum Love* (2003); *In Borrowed Shoes* (2006); *Beyond the Reach of My Chopsticks* (2011) all Blue Willow Press (San Francisco). Permission: from the author. **pp. 228–29.**

Ashbery, John (b. 28 July 1927 Rochester NY, r. New York NY) Credits: "A blue anchor" "I inch" "Too late" all from "37 Haiku" *Sulfur* 5 (1981). Bibliography: *A Wave* (Viking 1984); *Selected Poems* (Viking 1985). Permission: "A Blue Anchor," "I inch" and "Too Late" from *A Wave* by John Ashbery. Copyright © 1981, 1982, 1983, 1984 by John Ashbery. Reprinted by permission of Georges Borchardt, Inc., on behalf of the author, and of Carcanet Press Limited. **p. 91.**

Atwood, Ann (b. ?, d. ?) Credits: "dead center" *FP* 12:1 (1989). Bibliography: *Haiku: The Mood of Earth* (Atheneum, New York 1971); *My Own Rhythm: An Approach to Haiku* (Scribner, New York 1973); *Haiku-Vision in Poetry and Photogra-*

phy (Scribner, New York 1977). Permission: deceased, no known literary executor. **p. 121.**

Avis, Nick (b. 7 January 1957 London UK, r. Corner Brook NFL) Credits: "deep inside" *FP* 11:4 (1986); "freshly fallen snow" *WC* 8 (1983); "northern lights shimmer" *MH* 17:1 (1986); "she raises the hem" *You Aim to Love*; "the telephone" *MH* 15:3 (1984). Bibliography: *bending with the wind: haiku and other poems* (Breakwater 1993); *You Aim to Love* (BLP 1988). Permission: from the author. **pp. 104–5.**

Baatz, Ronald (b. 30 November 1947 Hackensack NJ, r. Catskill NY) Credits: "look at the red throat" *Mt. Tremper Haiku*. Bibliography: *Mt. Tremper Haiku* (Flypaper Press, New York 2000). Permission: from the author. **p. 204.**

Bachini, Annie (b. 23 July 1950 London UK, r. London UK) Credits: "day after day" PR 9 (1999). Bibliography: *The River's Edge* (Bare Bones Press, Frome UK 2003). Permission: from the author. **p. 188.**

Baker, Winona (b. 18 March 1924 Southey SK, r. Nanaimo BC) Credits: "moss-hung trees" *Clouds Empty Themselves*. Bibliography: *Clouds Empty Themselves* (Red Cedar Press, Nanaimo BC 1987); *Moss-Hung Trees* (Reflections, Gabriola BC 1992). Permission: from the author. **p. 113.**

Ball, Jerry (b. 16 December 1932 Lincoln NE, r. Walnut Creek CA) Credits: "spring breeze" *MDN* 660 (2004); "autumn evening" *The San Francisco Haiku Anthology*. Bibliography: (editor) *The San Francisco Haiku Anthology* (SW 1992); *Pieces of Eight* (self-published 2011). Permission: from the author. **p.140.**

Banwarth, Francine (b. 29 June 1947, Los Angeles CA, r. Dubuque IA) Credits: "sun dogs" WPA 2007; "the river freezes" HNH 2011. Permission: from the author. **p. 276.**

Baranski, Johnny (b. 1 May 1948 Chicago IL, r. Vancouver WA) Credits: "in the prison graveyard" *Just a Stone's Throw*. Bibli-

d. 27 January 2012 Dunedin New Zealand) Credits: "fog-filled harbour" *the taste of nashi* (ed. Nola Borrell and Karen P. Butterworth, Windrift Press, Wellington NZ 2008). Bibliography: *Beyond the Paper Lanterns: A Journey with Cancer* (Paper Lantern Press, Lower Hutt NZ 2000). Permission: from the estate of the author. **p. 283.**

Chula, Margaret (b. 10 October 1947 Brattleboro VT, r. Portland OR) Credits: "Hiroshima heat" *Grinding My Ink*; "night of the new moon" *The Smell of Rust*; "Through the slats" *MH* 18:3 (1987). Bibliography: *Grinding My Ink* (KP 1993); *The Smell of Rust* (KP 2003). Permission: from the author. **p. 112.**

Clark, Thomas A. (b. 16 April 1944 Greenock Scotland, r. Pittenweem Scotland) Credits: "a terse note" *Tussocks*. Bibliography: *Tussocks* (Moschatel Press, Nailsworth UK 2000). Permission: from the author. **p. 205.**

Clausen, Tom (b. 1 August 1951 Ithaca NY, r. Ithaca NY) Credits: "a rake in hand" HNH 2010; "lunar eclipse" *Growing Late* (SNP 2006). Bibliography: *Homework* (SNP 2000). Permission: from the author. **p. 272.**

Cobb, David (b. 12 March 1926 Harrow UK, r. Braintree UK) Credits: "a moment between" *A Leap in the Light*; "daffodil morning" "filling the grave" and "a bust of wet clay" *Jumping from Kiyomizu*; "sciatica" *BS* 8:2 (1998); "spring sunshine" *Spitting Pips*; "the old spin bowler" *BS* 9:3 (1999). Bibliography: *A Leap in the Light* (Equinox Press, Shalford UK 1991); (editor) *The Haiku Hundred* (IP 1992); *Jumping from Kiyomizu: A Haiku Sequence* (IP 1996); (coeditor) *The Iron Book of English Haiku* (IP 1998); *A Bowl of Sloes* (SNP 2000); *Business in Eden* (Equinox Press 2006); *Spitting Pips* (Equinox Press 2009). Permission: from the author. **pp. 138–39.**

Collins, Billy (b. 22 March 1941 New York NY, r. Winter Park

FL) Credits: "Innumerable" *She Was Just Seventeen*. Bibliography: *She Was Just Seventeen* (Modern Haiku Press, Normal IL 2006). Permission: from the author. **p. 273.**

Colón, Carlos (b. 23 April 1953 Shreveport LA, r. Shreveport LA) Credits: "closing arguments" *Too Busy for Spring* (HNA 1999); "overtaken" *HH* 10:3 (1997); "pointing" *RN* 3:1 (1996). Bibliography: *Clocking Out* (Tragg Publications, Shreveport LA 1996). Permission: from the author. **p. 161.**

Cone, Jon (b. 1 June 1955 Charfield UK, r. Iowa City IA) Credits: "the cloud-edge" *ANT* 6 (2003). Bibliography: *Enough Salt* (Curvd H&Z, Ottawa 2001). Permission: from the author. **p. 235.**

Constable, Susan (b. 18 January 1943 Calgary AB, r. Nanoose Bay BC) Credits: "rising river" *AC* 20 (2008). Permission: from the author. **p. 284.**

Corman, Cid (b. 29 June 1924 Roxbury MA, d. 12 March 2004 Kyoto Japan) Credits: "Dark morning" *OF* vol. 1; "Of one stone" *o/1*; "On the brim" *Nonce*. Bibliography: *OF* vol. 1 (Lapis Press, San Francisco 1990); *o/1* (Elizabeth Press, New Rochelle NY 1974); *Nonce* (Elizabeth Press 1965); *Nothing Doing* (New Directions, New York 1999); *The Next Thousand Years: The Selected Poems* (Longhouse, Guilford VT 2008). Permission: Longhouse Publishers. **p. 31.**

Crook, John (b. 8 December 1945 Watlington, Oxfordshire UK, d. 16 April 2001) Credits: "high tide" *BS* 11:2 (2001); "summer solstice" *HCal* 1999. Bibliography: *Ebb Tide: Selected Haiku* (SNP 2003). Permission: from the estate of the author. **p. 195.**

Cummings, E. E. (b. 14 October 1894 Boston MA, d. 3 September 1962 North Conway NH) Credits: "l(a" *95 Poems*. Bibliography: *95 Poems* (HB 1958), *Complete Poems, 1913–1962* (HB 1994). Permission: "l(a". Copyright © 1958, 1986, 1991 by the Trustees for the E. E. Cummings Trust, from *Complete Poems: 1904–1962* by E. E. Cummings, edited by George J. Firmage. Used by permission of Liveright Publishing Corporation. **p. 9.**

Davidson, L. A. (b. 31 July 1917 Roy MT, d. 18 July 2007 New York NY) Credits: "beyond" *HM* 5:3 (1972); "the surfboard" Mya Pasek Award, St. Louis MO (1985); "what to say?" *NC* 4:1 (1987). Bibliography: *The Shape of the Tree* (WCP 1982); *bird song more and more* (SWP 2003). Permission: from the estate of the author. **p. 58.**

Day, Cherie Hunter (b. 3 July 1954 Morristown NJ, r. Cupertino CA) Credits: "a skull no bigger" *THN* 6:5 (2004); "looking up" *THN* 8:1 (2006); "palominos" *Woodnotes* 23 (1994); "salt wind" HNH 2010; "talk of the war" *MH* 35:1 (2004); "termites" *MH* 44.2; "winding road" *MH* 43.1. Bibliography: *The Horse with One Blue Eye* (SNP 2006). Permission: from the author. **pp. 158–59.**

de Gruttola, Raffael (b. 15 May 1935 Cambridge MA, r. Natick MA) Credits: "lost in the lights" Boston Haiku Society News (1999). Bibliography: *Recycle / Reciclo: A Haiku Sequence* (Cordillera Press, Natick MA 1989); (with Wilfred Croteau) *Echoes in Sand: Haiga* (piXeLaRt, Upton MA 2000). Permission: from the author. **p. 191.**

Dickson, Charles B. (b. 14 June 1915 Marietta GA, d. 12 May 1991 Marietta GA) Credits: "dense fog" *Appalachian Twilight* (HC Sheet 1987); "November field" *MH* 18:3 (1987); "rain-swept parking lot" *MH* 22:2 (1991), "shrill midnight cries" *A Moon in Each Eye*. Bibliography: *A Moon in Each Eye* (AHA 1993). Permission: deceased, no known literary executor. **p. 115.**

Dillon, Mike (b. 29 May 1950 Seattle WA, r. Indianola WA) Credits: "accidental orchard" *RR* 3:4 (2008); "it doesn't matter" *MH* 41:1 (2010); "the beautiful nun" *MH* 38:3 (2007); "The last kid picked" *MH* 26:1 (1995). Bibliography: *The Road Behind* (RMP 2003). Permission: from the author. **p. 160.**

Diridoni, Susan (b. 30 August 1950 San Francisco CA, r. Kensington CA) Credits: "step back" *Issa's Untidy Hut* 19 (2011); "vows leap" *RR* X:3 (2010). Permission: from the author. **p. 302.**

Donegan, Patricia (b. 2 May 1945 Chicago IL, r. Chicago IL) Credits: "I lay down" *Without Warning*; "last night lightning" JAL 1987–88; "spring wind" *MDN* Contest 1998. Bibliography: *Bone Poems (Mini-Cantos)* (Chinook Press, Boulder CO 1985); *Without Warning* (Parallax Press, Berkeley CA 1990); (editor) *Haiku Mind: 108 Poems to Cultivate Awareness & Open Your Heart* (Shambhala, Boston 2008). Permission: from the author. **p. 119.**

Donleycott, Connie (b. 5 October 1953 Aberdeen WA, r. Bremerton WA) Credits: "crowd of umbrellas" *THN* 3:6 (2001); "lilt in her voice" *THN* 7:4 (2005). Permission: from the author. **p. 210.**

Dorsty, George (b. 31 August 1943 Northport NY, r. Yorktown VA) Credits: "low tide" BR 12.1 (2010). Permission: from the author. **p. 290.**

Drevniok, Betty (b. 17 December 1919 St. Louis MO, d. 6 March 1997 Ottawa ONT) Credits: "Morning coolness" *MH* 9:2 (1978). Bibliography: *Aware: A Haiku Primer* (Portal Publications, Bellingham WA 1981). Permission: from the estate of the author. **p. 81.**

Duhaime, André (b. 19 March 1948 Montreal QC, r. Gatineau QC) Credits: "migraine" *Haiku Canada Holographic Anthology* (2004). Bibliography: *Pelures d'oranges* (Éditions Asticou, Hull QC 1987). Permission: from the author. **p. 236.**

Dunlap, Curtis (b. 3 November 1957 Reidsville NC, r. Mayodan NC) Credits: "secluded highway" *MH* 35:1 (2004). Bibliography: *Running Barefoot: Haiku and Senryu* (self-published 2006). Permission: from the author. **p. 237.**

Dunphy, John J. (b. 8 December 1953 Alton IL, r. Godfrey IL) Credits: "on a plaque" *FP* 23:3 (2000). Bibliography: *Old Soldiers Fading Away* (Pudding House Publications, Columbus OH 2006). Permission: from the author. **p. 199.**

Easter, Charles (b. 17 August 1958 Kingsport TN, r. Trenton NJ) Credits: "close lightning" *FP* 21:1 (1999). Permission: from the author. **p. 185.**

Eigner, Larry (b. 7 August 1927 Swampscott MA, d. 3 February 1996 Berkeley CA) Credits: "glad to have" *Waters/Places/A Time*; "one of two nickels" and "politics" *Windows/Walls/ Yard/Ways*. Bibliography: *Waters/Places/A Time* (Black Sparrow Press, Santa Rosa CA 1983); *Windows/Walls/ Yard/Ways* (Black Sparrow, 1994); *The Collected Poems of Larry Eigner*, vols. 1–4 (Stanford University Press, Palo Alto CA 2010). Permission: From *The Collected Poems of Larry Eigner* edited by Curtis Faville and Robert Grenier. Copyright © 2010 by The Estate of Larry Eigner. All rights reserved. Used with permission of Stanford University Press, www.sup.org. **p. 108.**

Einbond, Bernard Lionel (b. 19 May 1937 New York NY, d. 14 August 1998 Forest Hills NY) Credits: "the white of her neck" *HM* 2:3 (1968). Bibliography: *The Tree As It Is: New and Selected Haiku Poetry* (RMP 2000). Permission: from the estate of the author. **p. 34.**

Elliott, David (b. 26 December 1944 Minneapolis MN, r. Factoryville PA) Credits: "among leafless trees" *Piedmont Literary Journal* 1:1 (1992). Bibliography: *Wind in the Trees* (AHA 1992). Permission: from the author. **p. 142.**

Evetts, Dee (b. 16 May 1943 Ware UK, r. Winchester VA) Credits: "after Christmas" "his fury" and "damp morning" *End-*

ber morning" HNH 2012. Bibliography: *a gate left open* (RMP 2009). Permission: from the author. **p. 295.**

Gallagher, D. Claire (b. 7 December 1941 Milwaukee WI, d. 17 July 2009 Sunnyvale CA) Credits: "a loon" *The Nether World*; "jet lag" *FP* 29:3 (2006). Bibliography: *The Nether World* (RMP 2009). Permission: from the estate of the author. **p. 264.**

Galmitz, Jack (b. 28 March 1951 New York, NY, r. Elmhurst NY) Credits: "under the pier" *Sky Theatre.* Bibliography: *Sky Theatre* (*ink!* literary e-zine, no place 2004); *A New Hand: Haiku* (Wasteland Press, Shelbyville KY 2006). Permission: from the author. **p. 246.**

Gates, Larry (b. 12 June 1942 Chicago IL, r. Purvis MS) Credits: "snake in the grass" *Haiku* (ed. Eric Amann, Toronto 1971); "passing whale's eye" JAL 1987–88; "sound of honking geese" *FP* 10:4 (1987). Bibliography: *In the Twinkling of an Eye* (self-published 1969). Permission: from the author. **p. 54.**

Gay, Garry (b. 28 March 1951 Glendale CA, r. Santa Rosa CA) Credits: "Along the way" Nature Company "Haiku of the Earth" Contest 1994; "Hunter's moon" *WN* 27 (1995); "Bird song" *FP* 11.2 (1988); "Navajo moon" HGH 2011; "Skunk skull" *FP* 18:2 (1995); "The shape of clay" *River Stones.* Bibliography: *The Long Way Home* (BB 1998); *River Stones* (SAK 1999); *Along the Way* (SNP 2000). Permission: from the author. **pp. 124–25.**

Gilbert, Richard (b. 28 March 1954 Westport CT, r. Kumamoto Japan) Credits: "a drowning man" *NO* 1 (2004); "as an and" *RR* 11:2 (2011). Bibliography: *Poems of Consciousness: Contemporary Japanese & English-language Haiku in Cross-cultural Perspective* (RMP 2007). Permission: from the author. **p. 240.**

Gilli, Ferris (b. 13 April 1943 Tifton GA, r. Marietta GA) Credits:

"ashes drifting" SHI (1998); "still no word" *SN* 12 (2006). Bibliography: *Shaped by the Wind* (SNP 2006). Permission: from the author. **p. 180.**

Gilliland, Robert (b. 14 December 1946 Galveston TX, r. Austin TX) Credits: "autumn wind" *MH* 28:3 (1997); "jack-knifed rig" *FP* 26:3 (2003); "morning bird song" *MH* 33:3 (2002). Bibliography: *mosquitoes and moonlight* (SAK 1999). Permission: from the author. **p. 175.**

Ginsberg, Allen (b. 3 June 1926 Newark NJ, d. 5 April 1997 New York NY) Credits: "Mayan head" [p. 209] and "The madman" [p. 211] from *Journals Mid-Fifties 1954–1958* by Allen Ginsberg and edited by Gordon Ball. Copyright © by Allen Ginsberg. Introductory material copyright © 1995 by Gordon Ball. "Moonless thunder" *White Shroud:* excerpt of 1 line from "221 Syllables at Rocky Mountain Dharma Center" ("Moonless thunder. . . .") from *Collected Poems 1947–1997*. Copyright © 2006 by the Allen Ginsberg Trust. Bibliography: *Journals Mid-Fifties 1954–1958* (1995); *Mostly Sitting Haiku* (PH 1978); *White Shroud: Poems 1980–1985* (HR 1986); *Collected Poems, 1947–1995* (HR 2006). Permission: Excerpt of 1 line from "221 Syllables at Rocky Mountain Dharma Center" ("Moonless thunder. . . .") from *Collected Poems 1947–1997* by Allen Ginsberg. Copyright © 2006 by the Allen Ginsberg Trust. Reprinted by permission of HarperCollins Publishers. Two haiku: "Mayan head in a . . ." and "The madman . . ." from *Journals Mid-Fifties 1954–1958* by Allen Ginsberg and edited by Gordon Ball. Copyright © 1996 by Allen Ginsberg. Introductory material copyright © 1995 by Gordon Ball. Reprinted by permission of HarperCollins Publishers. Three Haiku by Allen Ginsberg. Copyright © 2010 by Allen Ginsberg, used by permission of The Wylie Agency LLC. **p. 10.**

Gordon, Chris (b. 13 May 1966 Toronto ONT, r. Eugene OR) Credits: "a love letter to" and "I meet the twin she" *Cucumbers Are Related to Lemons*; "a purple evening" *RN* 4:1 (1997); "the hand" *An Apparent Definition of Wavering*; "the nickels from" *RR* 5:3 (2010); "where the lines end" *ANT* 5 (2002). Bibliography: *An Apparent Definition of Wavering* (self-published 2004); *Cucumbers Are Related to Lemons* (self-published 2009). Permission: from the author. **p. 172–73.**

Gorman, LeRoy (b. 7 August 1949 Smith Falls ONT, r. Napanee ONT) Credits: "between" *FP* 24:3 (2001); "in the silent movie" *The Haiku Hundred* (1992); "quiet graveyard" *MH* 31:2 (2000). Bibliography: *Glass Bell: Selected Haiku* (KR 1991); *Nothing Personal* (PR 2001); *Wind in the Keys* (HCP 1981). Permission: from the author. **p. 143.**

Gourlay, Caroline (b. 10 August 1939 London England, r. Knighton Wales) Credits: "again no word" *Lull before dark*; "daylight fading" and "without a full stop" *Crossing the Field*; "fog-bound road" *MH* 33:2 (2002); "unopened letter" *PR* 27 (2005). Bibliography: *Crossing the Field* (Redlake Press, Clun UK 1995); *Lull before dark* (BB 2005). Permission: from the author. **pp. 162–63.**

Grenier, Robert (b. 4 August 1941 Minneapolis MN, r. Bolinas CA) Credits: "except the swing" *Sentences*. Bibliography: *Sentences* (Whale Cloth Press, Iowa City IA 1978). Permission: from the author. **p. 84.**

Gurga, Lee (b. 28 July 1949 Chicago IL, r. Champaign IL) Credits: "an unspoken assumption" *NG* 2:3 (2010); "fresh scent" Haiku Summit Contest 1996; "from house" *FP* 17:2 (1994); "not the whole story" *FP* 33:2 (2010); "rows of corn" *KU* (1996); "spot of sunlight" *MDN* 1 (1990). Bibliography: *Measure of Emptiness* (PH 1991); *In and Out of Fog* (PH

12 (1992). Bibliography: *In the Margins of the Sea* (SNP 2000); *A Path in the Garden* (KP 2000); *Inside Out* (RMP 2010). Permission: from the author. **pp. 146–47.**

Higginson, William J. (b. 17 December 1938 New York NY, d. 11 October 2008 Summit NJ) Credits: "Holding the water" *HW* 3:2 (1970); "I look up" *MH* 2:1 (1970). Bibliography: (with Penny Harter) *The Haiku Handbook: How to Write, Share, and Teach Haiku* (McGraw-Hill 1985); (editor) *The Haiku Seasons: Poetry of the Natural World* (Kodansha International, Tokyo 1996); (editor) *Haiku World: An International Poetry Almanac* (Kodansha International 1996); *Ten Years' Collected Haiku* vol. 1 (FH 1987); *Upright in the Washout: a posthumous collection of the haiku of William J. Higginson* (RMP 2010). Permission: from the estate of the author. **p. 43.**

Hotham, Gary (b. 28 July 1950 Presque Isle ME, r. Scaggsville MD) Credits: "clouds move in" *SN* 3 (1998); "coffee" *CIC* 3:4 (1979); "deserted tennis court" *HM* 3.2 (1969); "distant thunder" and "waiting room quiet" *MH* 6:2 (1975); "evening loon call" *MDN* Contest (2002); "fog" *New World Haiku* 1:4 (San Fernando CA, 1974); "letting" *FP* 3:1 (1980); "she comes back" *Beloit Poetry Journal* 44:4 (Beloit WI, 1994); "yesterday's paper" *WC* 28 (1989). Bibliography: *Against the Linoleum* (Yiqralo Press, Laurel MD 1979); *As Far As the Light Goes* (Juniper Press, La Crosse WI 1990); *Before All the Leaves Are Gone* (Juniper Press 1996); *Breath Marks: Haiku to Read in the Dark* (Canon Press, Moscow ID 1999); *Spilled Milk: Haiku Destinies* (Pinyon Publishing, Montrose CO 2010); *Nothing More Happens in the 20th Century: Haiku Dangers* (Pecan Grove Press, San Antonio TX 2012). Permission: from the author. **pp. 40–42.**

Howard, Dorothy (b. 30 November 1948 Shawinigan QC, r. Aylmer QC) Credits: "clear winter sky" *ANT* 5 (1999). Bibliography: (editor) *Haïku: anthologie canadienne / Canadian Anthology* (Éditions Asticou, Hull ONT 1985); *The Photographer's Shadow* (KR 1999). Permission: from the author. **p. 196.**

Hoyt, Clement (b. 14 May 1906 Houston TX, d. 20 June 1970 Hot Springs AR) Credits: "A Hallowe'en mask" *AH* 1:2 (1963); "Leaves moil in the yard" *AH* 3:2 (1965). Bibliography: *County Seat* (*AH* Press 1966); *Storm of Stars: The Collected Poems and Essays of Clement Hoyt* (Green World, Baton Rouge LA 1976). Permission: deceased, no known literary executor. **p. 23.**

Hryciuk, Marshall (b. 23 August 1951 Hamilton ON, r. Toronto ON) Credits: "pulling the shutters" *RN* 10:4 (2006). Bibliography: *Zenosex: The Sex Haiku of Marshall Hryciuk* (Nietzsche's Brolly, Toronto 2011). Permission: from the author. **p. 265.**

Hughes, Langston (b. 1 February 1902 Joplin MO, d. 22 May 1967 New York NY) Credits: "Suicide's Note" *Vanity Fair* (25 September 1925). Bibliography: *Collected Poems* (Alfred A. Knopf, New York 1994). Permission: "Suicide's Note" from *The Collected Poems of Langston Hughes* by Langston Hughes, edited by Arnold Rampersad with David Roessel, Associate Editor, copyright © 1994 by the Estate of Langston Hughes. Used by permission of Alfred A. Knopf, a division of Random House, Inc. Any third party use of this material, outside of this publication, is prohibited. Interested parties must apply directly to Random House, Inc. for permission. Reprinted by permission of Harold Ober Associates Incorporated. **p. 7.**

Jewell, Foster (b. 21 July 1893 Grand Rapids MI, d. August 1984 Quincy IL) Credits: "Somewhere behind me" *Sand Waves.*

"The bottoms of my shoes" "the winter fly" (from a ms. beginning 1956 and published nearly in toto as *The Book of Haikus*); "Thunder in the mountains" *The Book of Haikus*. Bibliography: *The Book of Haikus* (Penguin, New York 2003). Permission: Reprinted by permission of SLL/Sterling Lord Literistic, Inc. Copyright © by The Estate of Jack Kerouac. **pp. 12-13.**

Kettner, M. (b. 11 May 1947 Grand Rapids MI, r. Seattle WA) Credits: "your hair" *ANT* 5 (2002). Bibliography: *Highku* (Lilliput Review Press, Pittsburgh PA 2002). Permission: from the author. **p. 215.**

Kilbride, Jerry (b. 25 February 1930 Denver CO, d. 3 November 2005 San Francisco CA) Credits: "between fugues" *One Breath* (HSA Anthology 1995); "body bag" *MH* 34:2 (2003); "cloudberries" *WN* 15 (1992); "from winter storage" *BS* 6:3 (1989); "lunar eclipse" *MH* 12:1 (1981). Bibliography: *Tracings* (Lily Pool Press, Northfield MA 2004). Permission: from the estate of the author. **pp. 92–93.**

Kirkup, James (b. 23 April 1918 South Shields UK, d. 10 May 2009 Andorra) Credits: "In atomic rain" *Haiku International Anthology* (Tokyo 2002); "the blood" *Dengonban Messages*; "walking in dead leaves" *Seeds from a Birch Tree* (ed. Clark Strand, Hyperion, New York 1998). Bibliography: *Dengonban Messages: Oneline Haiku and Senryu* (Kyoto 1981); (editor) *The Haiku Hundred* (IP 1992); *the last butterfly: a posthumous collection of the haiku of James Kirkup* (RMP 2009). Permission: James Kirkup Collection. **p. 99.**

Klinge, Günther (b. 15 April 1910 Berlin, Germany, d. 27 April 2009 Gauting, Germany) Credits: "Indian summer" *Day into Night*. Bibliography: *Day into Night: A Haiku Journey* (CET 1980). Permission: no known literary executor. **p. 85.**

horse" *HM* 5:2 (1971); "the daisies" *MH* 19:3 (1988). Bibliography: *More Light, Larger Vision* (AHA 1992). Permission: from the estate of the author. **p. 55.**

Lloyd, David (b. 9 May 1930 Montclair NJ, d. 6 March 2009 Williamstown NJ) Credits: "Moonlit sleet" *HM* 4:4 (1971). Bibliography: *The Circle: A Haiku Sequence with Illustrations* (CET 1974). Permission: from the estate of the author. **p. 57.**

Louvière, Matthew (b. 20 December 1930 Avery Island LA, d. 2 May 2003 New Orleans LA) Credits: "saying too much" *The Marsh*; "Through the weave" *MH* 18:1 (1987). Bibliography: *The Marsh and Other Haiku and Senryu* (*MH* Press 2001). Permission: no known literary executor. **p. 109.**

Lowell, Amy (b. 9 February 1874 Brookline MA d. 12 May 1925 Brookline MA) Credits: "Last night it rained" *PO* (1921); "Nuance" *Pictures of the Floating World*. Bibliography: *Pictures of the Floating World* (Houghton Mifflin, New York 1919). Permission: public domain. **p. 4.**

Lucas, Martin (b. 28 October 1962, Middlesbrough UK, r. Preston UK) Credits: "facing fine rain" *Bluegrey* (1994); "greener than autumn light" *Earthjazz* (2008); "long shadows" and "somewhere" *Darkness & Light* (1996); "the thyme-scented morning" *PR* 39 (2009). Bibliography: *Bluegrey* (Hub Editions, Spalding UK 1994); *Darkness & Light* (Hub Editions 1996); (coeditor) *The Iron Book of British Haiku* (IP 1998); (coeditor) *The New Haiku* (SNP 2002); *Earthjazz* (Ram Publications, Isleworth UK 2003); (editor) *Stepping Stones* (BHS 2007). Permission: from the author. **pp. 170–71.**

Luckring, Eve (b. 31 December 1962 Wilmington DE, r. Los Angeles CA) Credits: "behind the camera" *FP* 28:2 (2005); "centuries of whispers" *MH* 42.1 (2011); "in tune with" *MH* 43:3 (2012). Permission: from the author. **p. 250.**

Poulsbo WA) Credits: "silent Friends meeting" *THN* 4:8 (2002). Bibliography: *refuge: a posthumous collection of the haiku of Robert Major* (RMP 2008). Permission: from the estate of the author. **p. 225.**

Marcoff, A. A. (b. 30 December 1956 Tehran Iran, r. Leatherhead, Surrey UK) Credits: "the way" *PR* 8 (1998). Bibliography: *A Shade of Being* (Hub Editions, Spalding UK 2003). Permission: from the author. **p. 177.**

Martone, John (b. 22 April 1952 Mineola NY, r. Charleston IL) Credits: "before" and "daughter waters" *Gaura* (tel-let, Charleston IL 2007); "chimney swifts" *ksana*; "forest skull's" *forest skull* (tel-let 2007); "new" *around this stream* (tel-let 1999); "snow" *bindle* (tel-let 2005); "stand at" *RR* 3:2. Bibliography: *Dogwood & Honeysuckle* (RMP 2004); *Ksana* (RMP 2009). Permission: from the author. **pp. 200–202.**

Mason, Scott (b. 18 April 1952, Bay Shore NY, r. Chappaqua NY) Credits: "how deer" KU 2008; "the passenger pigeon" *Sharing the Sun* (HSA 2010). Permission: from the author. **p. 280.**

Massey, Joseph (b. 19 September 1978 Chester PA, r. Arcata CA) Credits: "television light" *Bramble.* Bibliography: *Bramble* (Hot Whiskey Press, Austin TX 2005). Permission: from the author. **p. 253.**

McClintock, Michael (b. 31 March 1950 Los Angeles CA, r. Clovis CA) Credits: "60 stories" *Light Run*; "dead cat" *HM* 5:2 (1971); "moonrise" *SN* 9 (2001); "pushing" *Maya*; "the dead" *MH* 4:3 (1973); "while we wait" *The Haiku Anthology* (ed. Cor van den Heuvel, Anchor Doubleday, New York 1974); "where three drowned" *Sketches from the San Joaquin.* Bibliography: *Light Run: Haiku and Senryu Poetry* (Shiloh Press, Los Angeles 1971); *Maya: Poems 1968–1975* (SO 1976); *Sketches from the San Joaquin* (Turtle

Light Press, Highland Park NJ 2009). Permission: from the author. **pp. 50–51.**

McClure, Michael (b. 20 October 1932 Marysville KS, r. San Francisco CA) Credits: "NOTHINGNESS" from *Rain Mirror*, copyright © 1999 by Michael McClure. Permission: By Michael McClure, from *Rain Mirror*, copyright © 1999 by Michael McClure. Reprinted by permission of New Directions Publishing Corp. **p. 254.**

McCotter, Clare (b. 25 May 1963, Kilrea Northern Ireland, r. Kilrea Northern Ireland) Credits: "clouds in a mare's eye" *Black Horse Running*. Bibliography: *Black Horse Running* (Alba Publishing, Uxbridge UK 2012). Permission: from the author. **p. 297.**

McDonald, Tyrone (b. 10 August 1972 New York NY, r. New York NY) Credits: "tunnel graffiti" *Modern Haiku* 42:2 (2011). Permission: from the author. **p. 298.**

mckay, anne (b. 29 April 1932 Ottawa ON, d. 4 March 2003 Vancouver BC) Credits: "a flame" *A Cappella*; "a rook" *In the House of Winter*; "deep into the rainy valley" *A Matter of Wings*; "my words" *Intermezzo*. Bibliography: *In the House of Winter* (WC 1987); *A Cappella* (Cacanadadada, Vancouver BC 1994); *A Matter of Wings* (WC 1996); *Intermezzo* (WC 1998). Permission: from the literary executor of the author. **p. 118.**

McMurtagh, Shawn (b. 17 November 1955 Washington DC, r. San Diego CA) Credits: "war" *RN* 10:3 (2005). Permission: from the author. **p. 251.**

Metz, Scott (b. 28 November 1976, Allentown PA, r. South Beach OR) Credits: "a / not / her" *MH* 38:3 (2007); "a child's drawing" *The Youngest Ones* (TP 2005); "meadow speaking" *A Sealed Jar of Mustard Seed* (*ANT* 9) (2009); "only american deaths" *MH* 40:1 (2009); "somewhere"

NO 5 (2007); "the city's moan" *MH* 40:2 (2009). Bibliography: *lakes & now wolves* (MHP 2012). Permission: from the author. **pp. 258–59.**

Montgomery, Scott (b. 30 May 1951 Ithaca NY, r. Seattle WA) Credits: "her silence at dinner" *WC* 6 (1982). Permission: from the author. **p. 103.**

Moore, Lenard D. (b. 13 February 1958 Jacksonville NC, r. Durham NC) Credits: "late summer" *FP* 26:2 (2003); "summer stars" *THN* 5:1 (2003). Bibliography: *A Temple Looming* (Word Tech Editions, Cincinnati OH 2008). Permission: from the author. **p. 232.**

Morden, Matt (b. 21 June 1962, Usk Wales, r. Carmarthen Wales) Credits: "mountain wind" *AC* 3 (1999). Bibliography: *Stumbles in Clover* (SNP 2007). Permission: from the author. **p. 189.**

Moss, Ron C. (b. 14 April 1959, Nowra New South Wales, r. Leslie Vale Tasmania) Credits: "bloodwood moon" *SHI* 2009; "record heat" *WW* 2009; "starry night" *SHI* 2006. Permission: from the author. **p. 270.**

Mountain, Marlene (b. 11 December 1939 Ada OK, r. Hampton TN) Credits: "a butterfly" *RR* 3:1 (2008); "old pond" and "less and less" *Pissed Off Poems and Cross Words*; "spin on dead" *NO* 2 (2005); "above the mountain" *WC* 19 (1986); "he leans" *Amoskeag* 1 (University of Southern New Hampshire, Manchester NH 1984); "on this cold" *Moment/moment/moments*; "one fly" *CI* 2:1 (1977); "pig and i" *FP* 2:3–4 (1979); "thrush song" *MH* 21:3 (1990); "wood pile" *MH* 7.4 (1976). Bibliography: *the old tin roof* (self-published 1976); *Moment/moment/moments* (BB 1978); *Pissed Off Poems and Cross Words* (self-published 1986). Permission: from the author. **pp. 68–70.**

Muldoon, Paul (b. 20 June 1951 near Portadown Northern Ireland, r. Princeton NJ) Credits: "A hammock at dusk" *Hay*; "Old burial ground" *MH* 35:3 (2004). Bibliography: *Hay* (Faber & Faber, London 1998); *Sixty Instant Messages for Tom Moore* (MHP 2005). Permission: Excerpt from *Hay* by Paul Muldoon. Copyright © 1998 by Paul Muldoon. Reprinted by permission of Farrar, Straus and Giroux, LLC. Reprinted by permission of Faber and Faber Ltd. Excerpt from *Sixty Instant Messages for Tom Moore* by Paul Muldoon. Copyright © 2005 by Paul Muldoon. Reprinted by permission of Modern Haiku Press. **p. 184.**

Murtha, H. Gene (b. 19 October 1955, Philadelphia PA, r. Ramapo NJ) Credits: "Berlin Wall" *THN* 6:9 (2004). Permission: from the author. **p. 244.**

Natsuishi, Ban'ya (b. 3 July 1955 Aioi Hyogo Japan, r. Fujimi Saitama Japan) Credits: "From the future" *A Future Waterfall*. Bibliography: *A Future Waterfall* (RMP 1999). Permission: from the author. **p. 198.**

Ness, Pamela Miller (b. 5 May 1951 Boston MA, r. New York NY) Credits: "after all these years" *FP* 21:2 (1998). Permission: from the author. **p. 178.**

Nethaway, Charles D. Jr. (b. 21 November 1943 Oklahoma City OK, r. Reston VA) Credits: "spring" *FP* 8:1 (1981). Permission: from the author. **p. 98.**

Neubauer, Patricia (b. 12 June 1922 Philadelphia PA, r. Coplay PA) Credits: "New Year's parade" *SSE* 4:1 (1997). Bibliography: *Beneath Bare Cherry Trees: Haiku for Winter* (self-published 1987). Permission: from the author. **p. 174.**

Newton, Peter (b. 7 May 1965 Detroit MI, r. Winchendon MA) Credits: "standing" *AC* 26 (2011); "the animal" *Welcome to the Joy Ride*. Bibliography: *What We Find* (Imaginary Press, Winchendon MA 2011); *Welcome to the Joy Ride* (Imaginary Press, 2013). Permission: from the author. **pp. 292–93.**

Noyes, H. F. "Tom" (b. 1918 Beaverton OR, d. April 2010 Politia Greece) Credits: "arguing a point" *MH* 18:1 (1987); "Monday morning" *Kô* (1991); "Religion aside" *PER* 2:2 (1999). Bibliography: *Between Two Waves* (Editura Leda, Constanţa Romania 1996); *Favorite Haiku* vols. 1–5 (RMP 1998–2002). Permission: deceased, no known literary executor. **p. 117.**

Nunn, Graham (b. 24 May 1971 Brisbane Australia, r. Brisbane Australia) Credits: "swinging the axe" www.anotherlost shark.com (2012). Permission: from the author. **p. 299.**

Olson, Marian (b. 18 May 1939 Bremerton WA, r. Santa Fe NM) Credits: "god or no god" *BR* 8:1 (2006); "river's song" PEN 2003; "scattering seed" *Songs of the Chicken Yard*; "stars" *FP* 25:2 (2002); "who was here first" and "whole" *Desert Hours*; "winter sun" *NO* 3 (2006). Bibliography: *Songs of the Chicken Yard* (Honeybrook Press, Rexburg ID 1992); *Desert Hours* (Lily Pool Press, Northampton MA 2007). Permission: from the author. **pp. 150–51.**

Painting, Tom (b. 1 April 1951, Rochester NY, r. Atlanta GA) Credits: "big sky" *AC* 16 (2006). Bibliography: *Piano Practice* (BRP 2004). Permission: from the author. **p. 257.**

Patchel, Christopher (b. 5 June 1953, Philadelphia PA, r. Mettawa IL) Credits: "night train" *FP* 27:1 (2004); "we turn" HNH (2011). Permission: from the author. **p. 238.**

Patrick, Carl (b. 2 July 1937 Houston TX, r. New York NY) Credits: "fireflies" GB 1998. Permission: from the author. **p. 182.**

Paul, Matthew (b. 29 September 1966 New Malden UK, r. Isleworth UK) Credits: "lifting mist" *PR* 33 (2007); "my train delayed" *SN* 7 (2001); "teals whistle" *CH* 1:2 (2007). Bibliography: *The Regulars* (SNP 2006); (with John Barlow) *Wing Beats: British Birds in Haiku* (SNP 2008). Permission: from the author. **p. 208.**

Pauly, Bill (b. 20 April 1942 Davenport IA, r. Dubuque IA)

Sandbach, John (b. 19 May 1948 San Francisco CA, r. Kansas City KS) Credits: "losing its name" *MH* 39:1 (2008). Bibliography: *Wrinkled Sea* (Hikoo Press, Kansas City MO 2002). Permission: from the author. **p. 278.**

Sanfield, Steve (b. 3 August 1937 Cambridge MA, r. Nevada City CA) Credits: "the earth shakes" *Wandering* (Shaman Drum, Berkeley CA 1992). Bibliography: *The Perfect Breeze* (Tangram, Berkeley CA 2010). Permission: from the author. **p. 149.**

Schwader, Ann K. (b. 23 February 1960 Sheridan WY, r. Westminster CO) Credits: "razored through" *RR* 2:3 (2007). Permission: from the author. **p. 275.**

Segers, Michael (b. 10 July 1950 Macon GA, r. Lakeland FL) Credits: "in the eggshell" *HM* 5:2 (1971). Permission: from the author. **p. 53.**

Shea, Martin (b. 1 July 1941 New York NY, r. Los Angeles CA) Credits: "bolted space" *New World Haiku* 1:3 (1974); "moths have come" and "when the suicide" *Across the Loud Stream*; "Moving" *HM* 6:1–2 (1974); "moving out tomorrow" *Waking on the Bridge*; "terminal" *SO* 3 (1975); "the long night" *MH* 4:3 (1973); "they wade in" *Shadows' Children*. Bibliography: *Across the Loud Stream* (SO 1974); *Waking on the Bridge* (RMP 2008); *Shadows' Children: Selected Poems 1* (Lembeth Hall, Los Angeles 2011). Permission: from the author. **pp. 60–61.**

Simpson, Sandra (b. 15 August 1958, Ohakea New Zealand, r. Tauranga New Zealand) Credits: "photos of her father" *NG* 1:1 (2009). Bibliography: *Breath* (Piwakawaka Press, Tauranga New Zealand 2011). Permission: from the author. **p. 287.**

Snyder, Gary (b. 8 May 1930 San Francisco CA, r. Grass Valley CA) Credits: "This morning" and "the boulder in the creek never moves," "Lookout's Journal," from *Earth House Hold*, copyright © 1969 by Gary Snyder. Bibliography: *The Back*

Swede, George (b. 20 November 1940 Riga Latvia, r. Toronto ONT) Credits: "alone at last" *MH* 25:2 (1994); "at the edge" *A Snowman, Headless* (Fiddlehead Poetry Books, Fredericton NB 1979); "at the height" *CI* 1:4 (1977); "dawn" *Endless Jigsaw* (Three Trees Press, Toronto ON 1978); "one by one" *CI* 4:2 (1980); "passport check" *CI* 2:4 (1978); "the son who" *Poetry Nippon* 81/82 (1988); "Turning everything" *CI* 5:3 (1981); "wildflowers" *THN* 12:1 (2010). Bibliography: *Almost Unseen: Selected Haiku* (BB 2000); *Joy in Me Still* (Inkling Press, Edmonton ALB 2010). Permission: from the author. **pp. 76–78.**

Sweeney, Patrick (b. 13 September 1954 Philadelphia PA, r. Misawa Japan) Credits: "Slow swing of willows" *RR* 4:1 (2009); "Sparrows lift" *FP* 27:1 (2004); "under the nitrogen blue sky" *RR* 4:3 (2009). Permission: from the author. **p. 239.**

Swist, Wally (b. 26 April 1953 New Haven CT, r. Amherst MA) Credits: "deep bend of the brook" *MH* 22:3 (1991); "dewy morning" *MH* 17:2 (1986); "heat lightning" *MH* 21:1 (1990); "mourning dove" *MH* 17:3 (1986); "shadow after shadow" *HUM* 7:1 (1996); "walking farther into it" *MH* 19:3 (1988). Bibliography: *Blowing Reeds* (Timberline Press, Fulton MO 1995); *The Mown Meadow* (Los Hombres Press, San Diego 1996); *The White Rose* (Timberline Press 2000); *The Silence Between Us: Selected Haiku of Wally Swist* (BB 2005). Permission: from the author. **pp. 110–11.**

Tagliabue, John (b. 1 July 1923 Cantu Italy, d. 31 May 2006 Providence RI) Credits: "A child looking at" *AH* 2:1 (1964). Bibliography: *The Doorless Door* (Grossman, New York 1970). Permission: from the estate of the author. **p. 30.**

Tauchner, Dietmar (b. 14 June 1972 Neunkirchen Austria, r. Puchberg Austria) Credits: "deep inside" *RR* 6:4 (2006); "gender god" *RR* 1:2 (2006); "new radio" KU 2012; "spring longing" *THN* 7:4 (2005). Bibliography: *as far as i can* (RMP 2010). Permission: from the author. **p. 247.**

tripi, vincent (b. 9 June 1941 Brooklyn NY, r. Greenfield MA) Credits: "Ah water-strider" *paperweight for nothing*; "Changing the swallowtail" HGH 1996; "Colouring itself" *FP* 14:3 (1991); "Deathbed" *THN* 5:11 (2003); "Her only nipple" *THN* 5:3 (2003); "In" *to what none of us knows*; "Not falling" *between god & the pine*; "Sun" *HUM* 5:4 (1995); "The shell I take" *WN* 9 (1991). Bibliography: *white* (SWP 1994); *. . . the path of the bird* (*HUM* Press, 1996); *between god & the pine* (self-published 1997); *monk & i* (*HUM* Press 2001); *paperweight for nothing* (TP 2006); *to what none of us knows* (TP 2012). Permission: from the author. **pp. 134–36.**

Trumbull, Charles (b. 17 May 1943 Flint MI, r. Santa Fe NM) Credits: "October dusk" *AC* 17 (2006); "such innocent questions" *RR* IX:1 (2009); "we follow the fence" *MH* 29:3 (1998). Bibliography: *between the chimes* (KR 2011). Permission: from the author. **p. 179.**

van den Heuvel, Cor (b. 6 March 1931 Biddeford ME, r. New York NY) Credits: "an empty wheelchair" and "tundra" *the window-washer's pail*; "changing pitchers" *FP* 14:1 (1991); "city street" *Five O'Clock Shadow* (SSA 2000); "end of the line" *BS* 4:3/4 (1987); "hot day" *MH* 39:3 (2008); "lingering snow" *Small Umbrella* (SSA 1995); "snow on the saddle" *sun in skull*; "the shadow in the folded napkin" *CI* 1:3 (1977); "the windy stars" *MH* 22:1 (1991). Bibliography: *sun in skull* (Chant Press, New York 1961); *the window-washer's pail* (Chant Press 1963); (editor) *The Haiku Anthology* (three editions: Doubleday Anchor, New York 1974; Simon & Schuster, New York 1986; WWN 1999); *A Boy's Seasons* (Single Island Press, Portsmouth NH 2010). Permission: from the author. **pp. 16–19.**

Vayman, Zinovy (b. 9 April 1947 Moscow Russia, r. Allston

MA) Credits: "Yom Kippur eve" *Geppo* XXXIII:5 (2008). Permission: from the author. **p. 282.**

Verhart, Max (b. 14 January 1944, Heerlen Netherlands, r. Den Bosch Netherlands) Credits: "out of the haze" *SHI* March 2006. Bibliography: *only the white* ('t schrijverke, Den Bosch 2008). Permission: from the author. **p. 262.**

Violi, Paul (b. 20 July 1944 New York NY, d. 2 April 2011 Cortlandt Manor NY) Credits: "Don't look at my face" *Hanging Loose Press* (1988). Permission: Reprinted from *Likewise* © 1988 by Paul Violi, by permisison of Hanging Loose Press. **p. xxxiv.**

Virgilio, Nicholas (b. 28 June 1928 Camden NJ, d. 3 January 1989 Camden NJ) Credits: "after the bell" *MH* 16:3 (1985); "autumn twilight" *HW* 1:1 (1967); "barking its breath" *MH* 19:2 (1988); "bass" and "lily" *AH* 1:2 (1963); "Easter morning" *AH* 4.1 (1966); "flag-covered coffin" *MH* 12:3 (1981); "fossilence" *Global Haiku* (ed. Randy M. Brooks and George Swede, IP 2000); "my dead brother" *HW* 3:2 (1970); "over spatterdocks" *MH* 15:1 (1984); "removing" *MH* 14:3 (1983); "spentagon" *MH* 17:3 (1986); "the sack of kittens" *HW* 1.1 (1967); "town barberpole" *The Haiku Anthology* (ed. Cor van den Heuvel, 2nd edition, Simon & Schuster, New York 1986). Bibliography: *Selected Haiku* (2nd edition, BLP 1988). Permission: from the estate of the author. **pp. 24–27.**

Vizenor, Gerald Robert (b. 22 October 1934 Minneapolis MN, r. Berkeley CA) Credits: "After the heavy rains" *Raising the Moon Vines*; "cedar cones" *Matsushima*. Bibliography: *Raising the Moon Vines: Haiku Poems* (Callimachus Press, Minneapolis MN 1964); *Matsushima: Pine Islands: Haiku* (Nodin Press, Minneapolis MN 1984). Permission: from the author. **p. 29.**

Wangchuk, Karma Tenzing (b. 15 October 1946 Los Angeles,

CA, r. Port Townsend WA) Credits: "the fallen" poem card 2010; "stone before" *Stone Buddha*; "waiting for me" *a motley sangha* (ed. Stanford M. Forrester, BRP 2005). Bibliography: *Stone Buddha* (tel-let, Charleston IL 2009); *Street/Shelter* (Minotaur Press, Port Townsend WA 2010). Permission: from the author. **p. 256.**

Welch, Michael Dylan (b. 20 May 1962 Watford UK, r. Sammamish WA) Credits: "after the quake" *FP* 13:1 (1990); "crackling beach fire" *THN* 6.11 (2004); "meteor shower" HGH 2000; "morning chill" *Haiku Troubadours* (ed. Ban'ya Natsuishi, Ginyu Press, Fujimi Japan 2000); "paper route" *MH* 26:3 (1995); "pulsing" *SN* 2 (1998). Bibliography: *For a Moment* (KR 2009), (editor) *Tidepools: Haiku on Gabriola* (Pacific-Rim Publishers, Gabriola BC 2011). Permission: from the author. **pp. 132–33.**

West, Harriot (b. 27 January 1945 Boston MA, r. Eugene OR) Credits: "dusk" *PR* 36 (2008). Permission: from the author. **p. 279.**

Wiggin, Larry (b. 15 November 1919 Northfield NH, d. November 1973 Tilton NH) Credits: "cleaning whelks" *Haiku* (Toronto); "crickets" *HM* 5:2 (1971). Permission: no known literary executor. **p. 56.**

Wilbur, Richard (b. 1 March 1921 New York NY, r. Cummington MA) Credits: "Sleepless at Crown Point" *The Mind-Reader*. Bibliography: *The Mind-Reader: New Poems* (Harcourt Brace Jovanovich, New York 1976), *Collected Poems* (Houghton Mifflin Harcourt, New York 2004). Permission: "Sleepless at Crown Point" from *The Mind Reader* by Richard Wilbur. Copyright © 1971, and renewed 1999 by Richard Wilbur. Reprinted by permission of Houghton Mifflin Harcourt Publishing Company. All rights reserved. **p. 71.**

Williams, Alison (b. 13 September 1957 Sleaford UK, r. South-
ampton UK) Credits: "long evening" *HP* 12 (2001); "mid-
day heat" *HP* 16 (2002); "trying to switch" *MH* 43:1 (2012).
Permission: from the author. **p. 209.**

Williams, Paul O. (b. 17 January 1935 Elsah IL, d. 2 June 2009
Livermore CA) Credits: "a cat watches me" *MH* 22:1 (1991);
"after the zinnias" *FP* 6:3 (1983); "from mud" *FP* 4:3 (1981);
"gone from the woods" *FP* 12.2 (1989); "tree" *San Francisco
Haiku Anthology* (SW 1992). Bibliography: *Tracks on the
River: 64 Poems* (Coneflower Press, Elsah IL 1982); *Outside
Robins Sing: Selected Haiku* (BB 1999). Permission: from the
estate of the author. **pp. 96–97.**

Willmot, Rod (b. 27 December 1948 Toronto ONT, r. Montreal
QC) Credits: "A page of Shelley" and "Listening" *Haiku*;
"the mirror fogs" and "the water stills" *Sayings for the Invis-
ible.* Bibliography: *Haiku* (Éditions Particulières, Quebec
1969); *Sayings for the Invisible: Haiku and Haiku Sequences*
(BMP 1977–87). Permission: from the author. **p. 48.**

Wills, John (b. 4 July 1921 Los Angeles CA, d. 24 September
1993 Sarasota FL) Credits: "a box of nails" *CI* 1:2 (1977);
"a snowy owl" *mountain* (1993); "boulders" *The Haiku
Anthology* (ed. Cor van den Heuvel, Doubleday Anchor,
New York 1974); "den of the bear" *The Haiku Anthology*
(ed. Cor van den Heuvel, Simon & Schuster Touchstone
2nd revised edition 1986); "the hills" and "mule" *Back
Country*; "this rock" *Reed Shadows*; "dusk" "rain in gusts"
and "the sun lights up" *up a distant ridge*; "going" and
"the moon at dawn" *river*; "keep out sign" *SO* 3 (1976);
"wildflowers" *BR* 4:2 (1986). Bibliography: *Weathervanes*
(Sangre de Cristo Press, El Rito NM 1969); *Back Country*
(Kenan Press, Statesboro GA 1969); *river* (Herald Com-
mercial Press, Statesboro GA 1970); *The Young Leaves*

(Georgia Southern College, Statesboro GA 1970); *Corn-stubble* (Georgia Southern College 1971); *up a distant ridge* (First Haiku Press, Manchester NH 1980); *Reed Shadows* (BLP 1987); *mountain* (S.E. Publishing, no place 1993). Permission: from the estate of the author. **pp. 44–47.**

Wilson, Billie (b. 1 August 1941, Lafayette IN, r. Juneau AK) Credits: "retreating glacier" *MH* 38:1 (2007); "storm warnings" Hawai'i Education Association Haiku Contest 2002; "whalebone" HGH 2003. Permission: from the author. **p. 227.**

Winke, Jeffrey (b. 20 March 1954 Milwaukee WI, r. Milwaukee WI) Credits: "blue dusk" *Janus–SCTH* 8:4 (1977). Bibliography: (editor) *Third Coast Haiku Anthology* (House of Words, Milwaukee 1978); *Coquette: Sensual Haiku* (Distant Thunder Press, Milwaukee 2008). Permission: from the author. **p. 79.**

Winters, Yvor (b. 17 October 1900 Chicago IL, d. 25 January 1968 Los Altos CA) Credits: "Winter Echo" *The Magpie's Shadow*. Bibliography: *The Magpie's Shadow* (Musterbookhouse, Chicago 1922); *The Poetry of Yvor Winters* (Swallow Press, Chicago 1978). Permission: public domain. **p. 6.**

Wright, Richard (b. 4 September 1908 Jackson MS, d. 28 November 1960 Paris France) Credits: "Coming from the woods" "In the falling snow" "Just enough of rain" "One autumn evening" "The indentation" "The sudden thunder" all from manuscripts 1958–60 selected and published as *Haiku: This Other World*. Bibliography: *Haiku: This Other World* (Arcade, New York 1998). Permission: Skyhorse Publishing Inc. **pp. 14–15.**

Yarrow, Ruth (b. 15 September 1939 Camden NJ, r. Seattle WA) Credits: "flash on the rim" and "my thumbprint" *Down Marble Canyon*; "a marmot's whistle" *MH* 10:2 (1979);

Haiku in English.